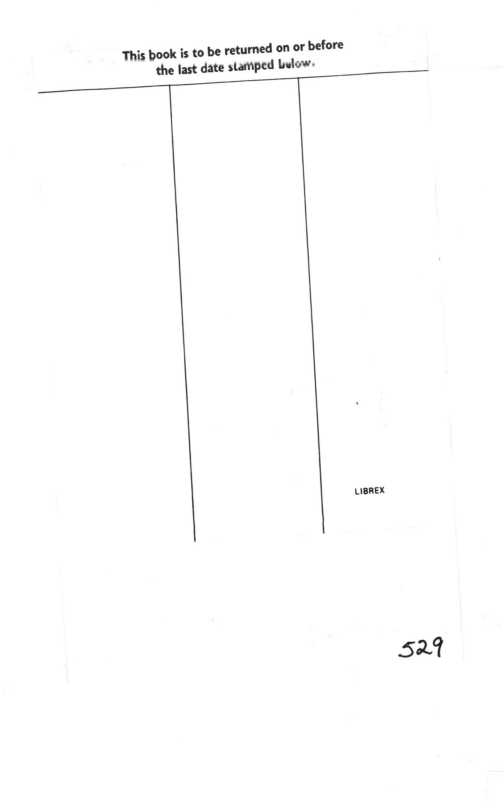

SCIENCE

THROUGH THE SEASONS

SUMMER

GABRIELLE WOOLFITT

Wayland

Titles in the series

Spring
Summer
Autumn
Winter

Series editor: Katie Orchard
Series designer: Pinpoint Design
Book designer: Jean Wheeler
Artist: Pauline Allen
Production controller: Carol Stevens
Photo stylist: Zoë Hargreaves

First published in 1995 by Wayland Publishers Ltd
61 Western Road, Hove, East Sussex, BN3 1JD, England

British Library Cataloguing in Publication Data

Woolfitt, Gabrielle
Summer. – (Science Through the Seasons series)
I. Title II. Series
507.8

ISBN 0 7502 1459 7

Typeset in England by Jean Wheeler
Printed and bound by L.E.G.O. S.p.A., Vicenza, Italy

Cover pictures: A green lizard, a butterfly on a buttercup and an electrical storm.
Title page picture: Deciduous woodland on a sunny day.

Contents

Words in **bold** are in the glossary on page 30.

What is Summer?

Summer is the hottest season of the year. Summer starts with the longest day of the year. This day is called the summer **solstice**. During the summer, daylight lasts longer than twelve hours and it is usually warm, even at night.

The sun can feel very hot in summer, so this family is having a picnic in the shade of a tree.

Swallow ▶

▼ Poppy

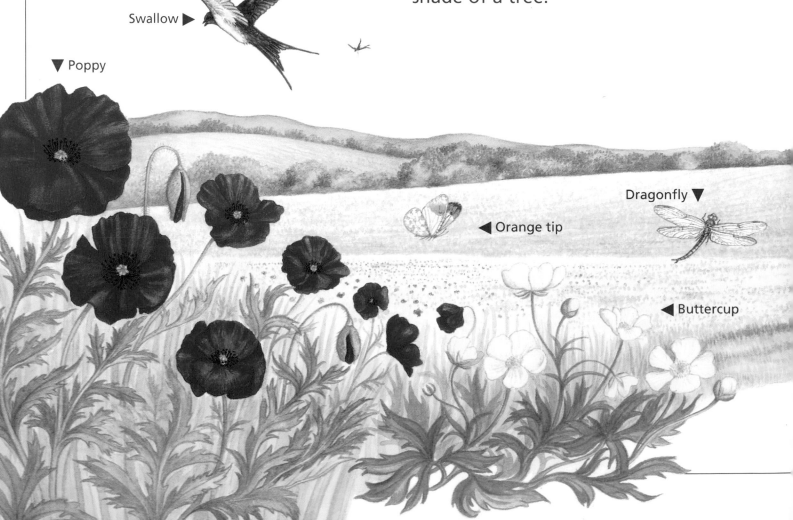

◀ Orange tip

Dragonfly ▼

◀ Buttercup

In the summertime, there are a lot of colourful flowers in parks and gardens. **Crops** become **ripe** in the fields. Animals find shade from the hot summer sun, while insects buzz around flowers in bloom.

Summer is a great time to be outside. Most people choose to go away on holiday in summer. Summertime ends on a day called the autumn **equinox**.

Great spotted woodpecker ◀

Horse chestnut ◀

Tree creeper ▶

◀ Nuthatch

Mayweed ▶

Clover ▶

Long, Hot Days

The earth has warmed up during the spring. There is still plenty of sunlight and it does not get dark until late evening. The hottest weather is often in the middle of summer when the land and the sea are already warm.

There are sometimes sudden, heavy thunderstorms in the late afternoon, but the rain is warm and soon clears up. In cities, summer can be a time of bad **air pollution**. The **fumes** from cars turn into poisonous chemicals in the sunlight. Some people get hay fever from the **pollen** made by flowers.

The sunlight helps fruit to ripen. By the end of summer, there will be plenty of fresh fruit on the trees.

◀ Tomato

Thunderstorms are common in summer. Lightning is a huge release of electricity.

Cherry ▶

▼ Apple

(Main picture) Some trees and shrubs that bear fruit in the summer.

Blackberry ▶

Summer Around the World

In the northern **hemisphere**, summer is from June to September. In the southern hemisphere summer is from December to March. Summer is not the same all over the world.

In the **poles**, there are twenty-four hours of daylight at the start of summer. As darkness never falls at this time, it is called the 'land of the midnight sun'.

These dark, juicy grapes have ripened in the hot Mediterranean sun.

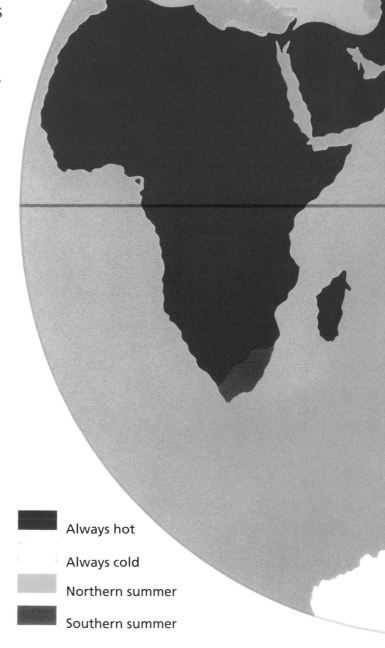

■ Always hot

□ Always cold

Northern summer

Southern summer

North Pole

Equator

South Pole

In the middle of **continents**, the land can become very hot because it does not have cooling wind from the sea. Alice Springs, in the middle of Australia, is hot all year round. In midsummer temperatures rise even higher and can reach above 40 °C. It hardly ever rains.

In places near the sea, the temperature does not get so high. The sea helps to keep the land cool.

The sandy path between the trees is a river bed in Namibia. It is dry because there is hardly ever any rain here.

Summer Sun

At the start of summer, the sun is almost directly overhead at midday. This experiment will show you how the sun moves across the sky during the day.

YOU WILL NEED:

some wool, a metre ruler, pencils, paper, two people.

1. On a sunny morning, stand outside in the middle of an open space and hold a metre ruler straight up.

▲ 2. Ask a friend to tie one end of the of wool to the bottom of the metre ruler and to pull the wool along its shadow, right to the end of the shadow.

▲ 3. Ask your friend to make a note of the time of day, the position of the sun in the sky, and the length of the shadow. Repeat the experiment every hour with a different piece of wool.

At the end of the day, look at your notes. When was the shadow the longest? When was the shadow the shortest? Where was the sun at these times?

At the start and the end of the day, the sun is low in the sky so the shadows are longer. At midday, the sun is high in the sky and the shadows on the ground are shorter.

A Day at the Beach

People often go on holiday to the beach when it is sunny. You may find shells, pebbles, or wood on the seashore. Some of these objects will **float** on the water. Other objects will **sink**. This experiment shows you which objects float in the sea and which objects sink.

▲ 1. Choose some objects that you think will float and place them gently in the basin of water. Were you right?

2. Repeat this with something large and heavy such as a stone. Does it sink or float? ▶

YOU WILL NEED:

some objects that you might find on a beach, such as shells, stones, some wood, sand, toys that you might play with in water, a basin of water.

▲ 3. Now try it with something small and light, such as sand. Would you expect it to sink or float?

Objects that are heavier than water will sink. Sand sinks because each tiny piece is heavier than the same tiny amount of water.

Keep Cool

Sunshine keeps us warm. But if it is too hot, we may get **sun stroke**. Our bodies work hard to help keep us cool.

Horses and dogs lose some of their hair in the summer so they do not get too hot. Farmers shear their sheep in summer. The sheep stay cool, and we can use the wool to make clothes.

Reptiles like this lizard use the sun's heat to get warm. They stay in the shade when it is very hot to keep cool.

Oak ▶

▲ Horses

Reptiles lie with their bodies in the sun in the morning to heat their bodies up. At the hottest part of the day, they face the sun or hide under cool rocks.

Dogs pant. This allows cool air to blow over their tongues. The moisture on their tongues **evaporates** and the air takes the heat from their bodies. Other animals lie in the shade to keep cool.

▲ Maple

Sheep ▶

Common lizard ▼

▼ Sand lizard

Labrador ▶

Cooling Down

If you get too hot, you need to cool your body down. This experiment shows you how to cool down.

YOU WILL NEED:

cotton wool, a cup of water, some baby wipes.

▲ 2. Wipe the back of your hand with a baby wipe.

▲ 1. Blow gently on your hand. What can you feel?

▲ 3. Blow on it gently again. Is it different from blowing on a dry hand?

▲ 4. Wet a piece of cotton wool and squeeze it out.

▲ 5. Wipe the back of your other hand with the wet cotton wool.

◀ 6. Blow on your wet hand again. How does it feel this time? Did air, or air and baby wipe, or air and water cool your hand down the most?

Your body cools down naturally when you sweat. Sweat is like the water in the experiment. Air makes the sweat evaporate off your skin and takes your body heat away.

Summer Flowers

In the summer, you can see many different types of flowers. All plants feed and reproduce in similar ways. These activities tell you more about plants.

▲ 1. Look at the pot plant. Draw the flowers, the leaves and the stems.

YOU WILL NEED:

a pot plant with flowers, a large bright flower, a white flower with a firm stem, some food colouring, a glass of water, coloured pencils, paper.

▲ 2. Dig gently around the soil at the base of the stems with your fingers. Can you see the roots?

The flowers, leaves, stems and roots are the main parts of a plant.

3. Look at the large open flower. Smell it. If it smells, it has **nectar** at the bottom of the petals. What do you think insects like about flowers?

Insects like to visit brightly-coloured flowers with sweet-smelling nectar.

▲ 4. Place the white flower in a glass of water with some food colouring.

◀ 5. After a day, look at the flower once more.

The petals have changed colour because water travels up the stem.

Summer On the Farm

▼ Crop sprayer

This wheat is ripe. Some of the crop has been **harvested**. The wheat can be used to make bread.

In summer, the crops ripen in the sunlight. The farmer must watch out for insects or animals eating the crops. Sometimes the farmer sprays the crops with **fertilizer** to help them to grow.

5 MAY

1923: Chanel No 5

The classic perfume went on sale in Paris. Gabrielle 'Coco' Chanel created it with chemist Ernest Beaux. Five was Chanel's lucky number and the perfume's sample number. Chanel No 5 was launched on the fifth day of the fifth month. The Chanel suit and 'little black dress,' have made Chanel a leader of 20th century haute couture.

1983: Cliff Young

Cliff Young was unknown as a runner and he was 'old.' Yet the 61-year-old won the inaugural Sydney to Melbourne Westfield Ultra-marathon. He ran 875 km in five days and fifteen hours. He ran with a 'shuffling' gait from training in gumboots on his Victorian farm. Network 10 created a Golden Gum Boot Award that Young received for 'Remarkable Athletic Achievement.'

2004: Maori Hikoi

15 000 mainly Maori protesters from 42 tribes marched 1,500 km to Wellington, New Zealand's capital. The two-week-long hikoi demanded that the federal government respect the 1840 Treaty of Waitangi's Maori claims to the seashore and beaches. Maori feared that if the law was changed, commercial development would soon follow.

1818 Karl Marx 'The father of modern communism' was born in Treves, Germany. He wrote *Das Kapital* and co-authored *The Communist Manifesto*. He died in London in 1883.

1862 Cinco de Mayo celebrations in Mexico and increasingly, worldwide, commemorate the French defeat by the outnumbered Mexicans under General Ignacio Zaragoza.

1891 Carnegie Hall was opened in New York City with a five-day festival conducted by Peter Tchaikovsky.

1902 The Prussian government, afraid that women would want to vote, banned all women's political groups.

1969 The first Pulitzer Prize for a book by a native American was awarded to N Scott Momaday for *House of Dawn*.

Fashion designer Karl Lagerfeld, actress Nicole Kidman and Director Baz Luhrmann attend the Chanel fashion show during Paris Fashion Week 2005.

Inset: A famous N5 jewel used by Nicole Kidman is one of the Coco Chanel jewels.

6 MAY

1937: Hindenburg Disaster

The German airship Hindenburg, the largest dirigible 'blimp' ever built, burst into flames at Lakehurst, New Jersey, killing 33 of its 97 passengers and crew. A spark probably ignited the hydrogen as the dirigible approached its landing station. The 'Titanic of the sky' and pride of the Third Reich had made ten previous trips as a passenger vehicle between Germany and the USA.

1954: Roger Bannister

The 25-year-old Oxford medical student broke the four-minute mile barrier. Running 3:59.4, Bannister beat the previous record of 4:01.4 held by Sweden's Hagg Gunder. Running the mile in less than four minutes was previously thought to be impossible, but just two months after Bannister broke the record, another runner, Australian John Landy, broke four minutes. The two runners faced off in Vancouver in a race called 'The Mile of the Century,' which Bannister won. Bannister went on to become an influential neurologist. He was knighted in 1975 for his inspirational achievement in running the 'miracle mile.'

1970: The South African Census

The census reported the following statistics:
Blacks 15 million
Whites 4 million
Coloureds 2 million (originally slaves who intermarried)
Asian 600 000.
Only whites could vote.

1994: Chunnel

Queen Elizabeth II and French President Francois Mitterand formally opened the Channel Tunnel, which connects Britain and Europe. The 31-mile tunnel took over eight years to build and is a major technological feat, costing billions to build. Twenty-three miles of the Chunnel is underwater. The high-speed rail link allows passengers to travel from one country to the other in twenty minutes without seasickness on the rough Channel crossing.

1856 Sigmund Freud was born in Freiberg, Moravia. He was the founder of psychoanalysis. His theories have enormous influence on Western culture. He died in London in 1939.

1968 Sorbonne University, Paris, closed for first time in its 700-year history because of violent student demonstrations.

1988 Zimbabwe's Graeme Hick was hailed as a cricket prodigy when the 21year-old scored 400 runs in one game.

1994 Marlene Dietrich died at 90 in Paris. In her time, she was the highest paid movie star and known for her 'bedroom eyes' and her affairs with leading men.

2002 Queen's Bohemian Rhapsody beat out the Beatles' **Imagine** and **Hey Jude** for top spot in the Top 100 British Singles Guinness poll.

Spring in Paris 1968: Parisian students and sympathisers parade in Montparnasse, demonstrating their opposition to government of President De Gaulle. Twelve million French workers went on strike for the same reason. The demonstrations turned ugly when French riot police tried to clear the the streets.

7 MAY

1840: Peter Ilich Tchaikovsky

The composer was born in Vatkinsk, Russia. He showed no particular aptitude during his early musical training, but after studying composition with Anton Rubinstein his creativity emerged in his early twenties. He was fortunate to have the mentorship of a wealthy widow, Nadezhda von Meck, who helped him both emotionally and financially. He was plagued with unhappiness and difficulties concealing his homosexuality and committed suicide in 1893. His most famous opera was *Evgeny Onegin* and his symphonies include the *1812 Overture*. Tchaikovsky's ballets include *Sleeping Beauty*, *The Nutcracker* and *Swan Lake*.

1901: Gary Cooper

The iconic cowboy movie star was born in Helena, Montana. He won two Oscars for *Sergeant York* and *High Noon*. He was a travelling salesman when friends told him that Hollywood was looking for men who could ride horses, so he applied to be an extra. He launched his major acting career in *The Virginian*. He said that 'Yup' was a convenient word, as it discouraged fans' and the media's personal questions. He never thought much of himself as an actor and refused to play Shakespeare as he said he would look stupid in tights. In 1939, the US Treasury announced that Cooper was the nation's top wage earner. In April 1961 Cooper won a special career-achievement Oscar. He died of cancer the following month age 60.

1915: Lusitania

A German submarine torpedoed the world's largest passenger liner, Britain's *Lusitania*, off the Irish Coast, killing 1198. Another 764 were rescued. Angry British mobs attacked German owned stores. The incident swayed US public opinion, as 124 Americans died and the United States eventually entered World War 1. Recruitment posters stated: 'Remember Lusitania!' .

1189 Hamburg, Germany was established as a free city. It is celebrated as Hafengeburtstag.

1663 The first Theatre Royal was opened on London's Drury Lane.

1765 HMS Victory, the flagship of Lord Nelson was launched. It is preserved and on exhibit at Portsmouth.

1824 Beethoven's 9th Symphony was first performed under his baton, despite his complete deafness.

1833 Johannes Brahms, pianist and composer, was born in Hamburg, a leading figure in German Romantic music, known especially for his *Requiem*.

1944 Richard O'Sullivan star of *Dick Turpin* and TV sitcoms was born in London.

American actor Gary Cooper, the film version of a cowboy, who thought he would 'look stupid in tights'.

1828: Jean Henri Dunant

The Swiss humanitarian and philanthropist, was born in Geneva. When he saw injured soldiers left writhing on the battlefield in the 1859 war between Napoleon Bonaparte's French army and the Austrians, he was appalled. The horrors of war were indelibly etched in his brain and he wrote a book about what he had seen, *Memories of Solferino*. In 1894 Dunant helped established the Red Cross Society and the Geneva Convention. His book was re-issued as the *Origin of the Red Cross*. He shared the first ever Nobel Peace Prize in 1901. At the time of his death in 1910, his organisation was the world's largest and best known humanitarian organisation.

1884: Harry S Truman

The 33rd US President, a Democrat, was born in Missouri. He learned leadership skills in the artillery in World War 1. On his return from combat he became a haberdasher and entered local politics. His political ascendancy and success as president surprised many. He had big shoes to fill when he succeeded F.D. Roosevelt, who died in office during the Second World War. Truman was nicknamed 'Give 'Em Hell, Harry' for his bluntness. He had only been in office for three months when he decided to use the hydrogen bomb to end the War in the Pacific. Truman had a fairy-tale lifelong romance with his wife Bess whom he fell in love with when he was five-years-old, in Sunday School. His views on child-rearing were, 'The best way to give advice to your children is to find out what they want and advise them to do it.'

1992: Miss Namibia

Michelle McLean was the first Namibian crowned Miss Universe from among seventy-eight contestants. She was a 6-foot tall model and professional masseuse. Australia's Georgina Denahy was a semi-finalist.

1794 Antoine Lavoisier, 'The father of modern chemistry' was guillotined, age 50, for his role as a tax collector. His major work was on combustion.

1896 The first horseless carriage (car) show was held at London's Imperial Institute.

1926 David Attenborough the naturalist, author and popular TV host was born in London.

1937 Edgar Bergen the ventriloquist and his blockhead, Charlie McCarthy premiered on their own US radio show.

1945 VE Day: The day of victory for Europe and her Allies in WWII.

1971 Rolling Stones album Sticky Fingers topped the UK charts. The cover, designed by pop artist Andy Warhol, featured a real zipper on a pair of jeans.

Sir David Attenborough's outstanding career in broadcasting spans more than 50 years. He started at the BBC in 1952 and began his famous *Zoo Quest* series in 1954. He travelled to the wilder parts of the world for the next ten years. Many other programs, including *Life on Earth*, and documentary films followed that have made him a household name around the world.

1850: Sir Thomas Johnstone Lipton

Born in Glasgow, Scotland on this day, Lipton went from errand boy to millionaire by the age of 30. He founded Lipton's grocery chain and Lipton's Tea, boxes of which bear his picture and invented the tea bag. Lipton was an avid sportsman. After losing in the America's Cup for the fifth time in 31-years he was given a gold cup for good sportsmanship. Lipton died in 1931 and left much of his fortune to the city and people of Glasgow.

1901: Australian Parliament

Australia's first Federal Parliament opened. The states had been colonies until 1 January 1901 when they federated into one nation and held federal elections. Parliament's opening was a spectacular event befitting a new nation. It was held in Melbourne's Royal Exhibition Building, with about 13 000 guests, including the parliamentarians, academics, consuls and military and naval officers. The Duke and Duchess of Cornwall (later King George V and Queen Mary) represented Great Britain.

1983: Philippe Jeantot

The French yachtsman won the BOC Solo Challenge in *Credit Agricole*. It was the first organised single-handed boat race round the world. He broke the previous record with a time of 159 days, 2 hours 26 minutes and 1 second. He topped this achievement in the 1987 race, in 134 days. Jeantot founded the Globe challenge-a nonstop race around the world. He came in fourth, in a whisker under 114 days. In the early 1990s, Jeantot competed in his final BOC Challenge and took third place with a time of 129 days. Jeantot retired as one of the legendary solo yacht racers, to resume his boat business in France.

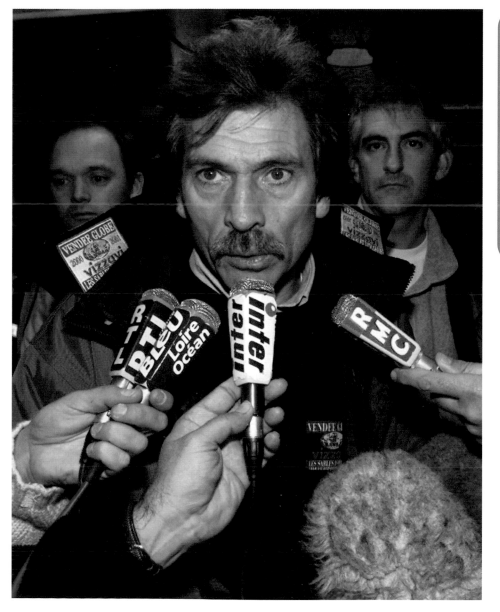

1928 Richard 'Pancho' Gonzalez, two-time US national amateur champion tennis player was born in Los Angeles. He was a crowd-pleaser who popularised the game.

1932 London's Piccadilly Circus' advertising signs were lit with electricity for the first time.

1936 Actor Albert Finney was born in Manchester, England. He is known for *The Dresser* and *Tom Jones*.

1937 Actress Glenda Jackson was born in Birkenhead, England. She won two Oscars, for *Women in Love* and *A Touch of* Class. She became a Member of Parliament in 1992.

Philippe Jeantot, organizer of the 'Vendee-Globe' solo round-the-world race.

10 MAY

1960: Bono

Rock band U2's lead singer, Paul Hewson, was born in Dublin. He changed his name to Bono from a billboard advertisement for Bona Vox hearing aids, which is Latin for 'good voice'. In 2004 he received the International Freedom Award from the National Civil Rights Museum for promoting western involvement in improving medical care and reducing poverty in Africa. He recommended that the World Trade Organisation and World Bank forgive their African loans and was nominated for a Nobel Peace Prize in 1995.

1996: Everest Claims Eight

In Mount Everest's worst climbing disaster, eight climbers died near the summit. Jon Krakauer, who was climbing with the group, wrote a book about the tragedy *Into Thin Air*. The dead included two of New Zealand's best alpinists, Rob Hall and Andy Harris. Hall had reached the summit five times, guiding 39 clients between 1990 and 1995. Knowing he would not survive the night, Hall said goodbye by radio to his pregnant wife Dr. Jan Arnold, herself an alpinist, in New Zealand. Toronto physicist Kent Moore studied the accident and theorised that 'the sky fell below them.' He said that weather patterns led to the stratosphere dropping onto the summit, which effectively made Everest 500 metres 'higher,' in terms of oxygen availability. The 75 mph winds contributed to the problem. A weather station placed on Everest in 1998 confirmed the theory when it recorded a 16-millibar fall in pressure.

1999: Quentin Blake

The first UK Children's Laureate award, won by Blake, was suggested by former Poet Laureate Ted Hughes. It celebrates an author or illustrator's lifetime achievement in the field of children's literature. The Laureate is an Ambassador for children's literature for two years. Blake has illustrated almost 300 books, for Roald Dahl (described as a 'partnership made in Heaven' for *The BFG*, *The Twits* and *The Witches*), Russell Hoban, Joan Aiken and many others. He has been illustrating since childhood and created his own characters, Mister Magnolia and Mrs Armitage.

1869 A ceremonial spike was driven into the tracks to connect two railway lines from the USA's East and West Coasts. The railroad was devastating to the Plains Indians, because it brought settlers and hunters and separated the buffalo herds.

1940 Jimmy Dorsey and his Orchestra recorded one of the first English versions of Alberto Dominguez's 1939 haunting *Perfidia* for Decca.

1978 Aldo Moro One of Italy's longest serving Prime Ministers and intellectuals was buried. He was kidnapped 55 days earlier and murdered by the Red Brigades.

1979 The Federated States of Micronesia was established. It includes the Pacific island nations of Yap, Pohnpei, Chuuk and Kosrae. It is a national holiday.

1999: Shel Silverstein the much loved US children's author died age 66. He wrote *A Light in the Attic*, *The Giving Tree* and *Where the Sidewalk Ends*. His humourous subjects included overdue library books, Brussels sprouts, folding umbrellas that devour people, shadows and the weather.

The body of the former Italian Prime Minister and Christian Democrat leader Aldo Moro (1916 – 1978) is found in the back of a van in Rome.

11 MAY

1904: Salvador Dali

The surrealist and cubist painter was born in Figueras, Spain and influenced by the 15th century artist Hieronymous Bosch. His themes were dreamy and bizarre, with time, memory and religion as subjects. Dali had a fetish for crutches, eyes and noses and was known for his trademark moustache and eccentric lifestyle. As well as painting he worked in film including with directors Luis Bunuel and Alfred Hitchcock. He said, 'There is only one difference between a madman and me. I am not mad.'

1981: Bob Marley

The influential Jamaican reggae musician and world icon died at the age of 36. Marley was born in 1945 to an English father and Jamaican mother. The Rastafarian spent some of his childhood in the Jamaican Trenchtown ghetto and his work centred on the oppressed. Through his songs, he brought a message of peace and brotherhood to the world. Marley, with 'The Wailers', helped create ska, rocksteady and reggae. In 1976 shots were fired into his home, lightly injuring him and his wife Rita, but his manager Don Taylor was critically injured. Marley was diagnosed with skin cancer, under a toenail in 1977, but refused to have the toe amputated. That was inconsistent with Rastafarian principles. He later underwent surgery, but the cancer had invaded his brain and Marley was too ill to return home to Jamaica. In April 1981, he received Jamaica's Order of Merit Award. Besides being a visionary, gifted songwriter and virtuoso, Marley is also credited with being the 'First Third World Superstar.'

1927 Comedian **Mort Sahl** was born in Montreal. He starred in *Don't Make Waves*.
1943 Over **10 000 US soldiers** landed on the remote Aleutian Island of Attu that had been occupied by the Japanese for five months.
1956 The **British Colonial Secretary** announced that the Gold Coast (now Ghana) would become the first independent black African nation.
1971 The UK's oldest tabloid, *The Daily Sketch*, founded in 1909, was published for the last time.
1981 Andrew Lloyd Webber's musical *Cats* premiered. It was based on TS Eliot's *Old Possum* poems. It became the longest running musical, closing in 2002.
1994 South African President **Nelson Mandela** named his chief political rival, Zulu Chief Mangosuthu Buthelizi, to his Cabinet.

Jamaican Reggae musician, songwriter, and singer Bob Marley performs on stage, in a concert at Grona Lund, Stockholm, Sweden, in 1978.

12 MAY

1937: King George V1
The King of England was crowned in Westminster Abbey. He was born in 1895. A retiring and shy man, he never expected to be King and only did so when his brother Edward abdicated to marry divorcee Wallace Simpson. The King won his subjects' affection during the Second World War when he refused to move from Buckingham Palace in downtown London during the Blitz. His daughter, Elizabeth, succeeded him after his death in 1952.

1967: John Masefield
The English poet laureate from 1930, died. He enjoyed a life at sea in his youth and wrote prolifically, often with nautical themes. His poetry anthology *Saltwater Ballads* includes 'I must go down to the sea again.' He wrote more than 50 volumes of verse and novels, such as *Dead Ned* as well as novels for children including *The Midnight Folk* and *The Box of Delights*.

1975: Jonah Lomu
New Zealand's former All Black Rugby Union player was born in Tonga. He was raised in New Zealand. He spent many years in his youth in trouble with police. Rugby turned his life around. By 1994 he was a World Cup All Black star. At his peak, Lomu could run 100 metres in 10.8 seconds. He won 60 international caps and scored 37 international tries. Before he played he had special rituals: he shaved his head and he ate a pre-match meal of mashed potatoes, spaghetti and six egg whites. Offered multi-million dollar deals to play overseas, he turned them down. He suffers from nephrotic syndrome, a kidney disorder, and had a transplant in 2004.

1820 Florence Nightingale the founder of modern nursing was born in Florence Italy. Using new techniques of statistical analysis during the Crimean War, she plotted the incidence of preventable deaths in the military. She developed the 'polar-area diagram' to dramatise the needless deaths caused by unsanitary conditions and the need for reform.

1978 Hurricanes were now named for men as well as for women.

1997 Russian President Boris Yeltsin and Chechen leader Aslan Maskhadov signed a peace treaty to end 400 years of conflict. The violence continues.

2001 Simon Raven the novelist, wit and hedonist died in London. He is best known for his 10 volume *Alms for Oblivion*.

2001 Perry Como the crooner died aged 87. He was known for 'Catch a Falling Star'.

Chechen separatist leader Aslan Maskhadov, who signed a peace accord with Boris Yeltsin, raises his fist in Grozny, capital of the breakaway southern republic of Chechnya. Maskhadov was elected president of Chechnya in 1997. Just months later Russia said it no longer recognized his legitimacy and sent more troops in October 1999. Maskhadov was killed by Russian troops on 8 March 2005, the third pro-independence president of the Muslim republic to be killed by Moscow. His death follows the killings of the first Chechen president, Djokhar Dudayev and his successor Zelimkhan Yandarbiyev in 2004 in Qatar.

13 MAY

1917: Children's Fatima Vision

Three children claimed they saw a vision of the Virgin Mary in Fatima, Portugal. Lucia Santos and her two cousins, Jacinta and Francisco Martos said they saw the Virgin Mary. On the thirteenth day of every month for six months, they claim the vision re-appeared and the Virgin Mary made cryptic revelations to them. The children were imprisoned for their 'heresy'. After an investigation the Roman Catholic Church called their visions 'worthy of belief.' Millions of people made pilgrimages to Fatima, which is now a revered site for the religious.

1950: Stevie Wonder

The enduring musician was born in Saginaw, Michigan. In 1963, the then 13-year-old, 'Little Stevie Wonder' became the youngest singer to top the US charts with his 'Fingertips Part 2'. He has been blind since birth, possibly because of over-oxygenation as a premature baby. Wonder's hero was the late Ray Charles and his first two albums when he was 12-years old were dedicated to him. They featured piano, harmonica and percussion. His genius emerged with hits like 'For Once in My Life' and 'Signed, Sealed, Delivered (I'm Yours)'. He toured with the Rolling Stones in 1972 and produced hit after hit, including 'You Are the Sunshine of My Life'. His music reflects elements of soul, R&B, funk, rock and roll, reggae, Africa and Broadway. His lyrics range from romance, to politics, to the ghetto. His most popular song, 'I Just Called to Say I Loved You', won an Oscar.

2002: Ruth Cracknell

One of Australia's favourite actresses died age 76 in Sydney. She had been a radio, revue, stage, TV and movie actress for 56 years. She had many nicknames—including Crackers, Dame Crackers and St. Ruth. Audiences especially loved her casting as Maggie Beare, the mother, in *Mother and Son*, a long-running ABC TV sit-com. She received many awards, including a Member of the Order of Australia, in 1980.

1788 The First Fleet of ships carrying British convicts left England for the new penal colony 'bound for Botany Bay.'

1914 RE (Tip) Foster, the only man to captain English teams in both cricket and football died of diabetes at age 46.

1927 Critic Clive Barnes was born in London.

1989 Jackie Mann, age 74, a Battle of Britain war hero and 40-year resident of Beirut, Lebanon, was kidnapped by rebels. He was released two years later.

1995 British climber Alison Hargreaves reached the summit of Mount Everest.

Ruth Cracknell, the leading lady of Australian theatre, television and film, talks to the media in Sydney in 1994

14 MAY

1969: Cate Blanchett
The actress was born in Melbourne. She graduated from Australia's prestigious National Institute of Dramatic Art. She has had major roles in theatre, television and movies with her first major success coming in *Oscar and Lucinda*. In 1998, her portrayal of *Elizabeth I* earned her an Academy Award nomination and her 2005 depiction of Katharine Hepburn in *The Aviator* earned her a Grammy and an Academy Award for Best Supporting Actress.

1997: Susie Maroney
The Australian long-distance swimmer became the first person to swim unassisted from Cuba to Florida. Fifty other swimmers had tried before and Maroney anticipated a swim of 45 hours. The temperature and currents were favourable and she arrived in just over 24 hours. In 1988, she swam from Mexico to Cuba in 38 hours and 33 minutes and then dined with Fidel Castro.

2003: Mary Donaldson
The 31-year-old Tasmanian married Denmark's Crown Prince Frederik in Copenhagen. They met during the Sydney Olympics. She is often compared with Jackie Kennedy Onassis for her understated elegance.

2003: Michael Morpurgo
Born in St. Albans, Hertfordshire, England in 1943, Morpurgo was appointed the 3rd UK Children's Laureate, a two-year appointment. He became a writer when he was a primary school teacher and needed a new story to read to the children every day. Morpurgo and his wife also administer three farms where inner-city children can stay for a week and learn about the countryside first-hand. Some of his books are *Gentle Giant, A Visit to the Farm* and *Wombat Goes Walkabout*.

1870 First Rugby Union Game played in New Zealand. They were called All Blacks from 1905, either because of their black jerseys or because of a typographical error where the reporter had described them as 'so fast they were all backs.' A printer added the letter 'l.'

1883 Australia's pioneering Duracks began driving their cattle herd from Queensland to the Kimberley in 1883. It took two years. Dame Mary Durack wrote an epic novel of life in The Kimberley, *Kings in Grass Castles*.

1944 George Lucas the visionary movie-maker was born in Modesto, California.

1952 David Byrne punk music pioneer of the Talking Heads, born in Dumbarton, Scotland.

2004 Bohol, Philippines, home of the world's smallest monkey, was inscribed as a World Heritage Site.

A tiny tarsier perches on a tree branch at a forest reservation in Corella, on Bohol island in the central Philippines. The tiny, tree-dwelling mammals, sometimes called the world's smallest monkeys, are being driven to extinction by the destruction of the country's forests.

15 MAY

1928: Flying Doctor

Australia's Royal Flying Doctor Service began operating from remote Cloncurry, Queensland, with the help of Qantas. Later the service moved to Central Australia. The Royal Flying Doctor Service (RFDS) combined innovations in medicine, aviation and radio to bring not only emergency care, 365 days a year, 24 hours a day, but comprehensive health to inland residents, over seven million square kms of country. At first, radios were foot operated. For everyday ailments, a doctor might relay first-aid instructions, referring to the RFDS manual and first-aid kit. For serious cases a doctor would fly to the patient, landing on a desert runway guided by bonfires. Seriously ill patients would be taken to hospital. In 2003-04 it tended 46 000 patients.

1935: Southern Cross Hijinks

Australian pioneer aviators Charles Kingsford 'Smithy' Smith and Patrick Taylor were delivering mail from Australia to New Zealand, when the *Southern Cross* developed engine trouble. Taylor climbed out under the wing and transferred oil from one engine to the other! Taylor had flown with Smithy on the first west-east crossing of the Pacific Ocean in the *Lady Southern Cross* in 1934. Both were knighted. Taylor died in 1966. Kingsford Smith was the first aviator to successfully circumnavigate the world.

1940: Nylon Stockings

Dupont synthetic nylon stockings went on sale for the first time in New York City. From May to December, sixty-four million pairs were sold. The stockings had seams down the back and were held up by a garter belt. When the USA entered World War II their sale was curtailed. The nylon was diverted to the war effort, where it was used for parachutes, tents and military clothing.

1996: Atal Bihari Vajpayee

The right wing leader became India's first Hindu Nationalist prime minister after Bharatiya Janata. His Bharatiya Janata Party emerged as the largest party in a hung parliament. He failed to form a coalition and resigned after 13 days. Vajpayee was re-elected in 1998 and continued free market reforms and India's nuclear program until 2004. He is a poet as well as a politician.

1730 Robert Walpole became Great Britain's first Prime Minister. Previously, the chief executive was known as the Chief Minister.

1811 Paraguay became independent from Spain.

1903 London's first electric tram service was opened by King Edward VII.

1932 An attempted coup took place in Tokyo, killing the Prime Minister. It led to a more influential military, with grave implications for China and the world.

1991 Edith Cresson became the first female French premier. She was a Socialist and served until 1992.

Above: Southern Cross, Charles Kingsford Smith's famous aeroplane.
Left: Pilot Sir Charles Kingsford Smith (1899–1935) and co-pilot Gordon Taylor shaking hands on their aeroplane the Southern Cross.

16 MAY

1763: Diary Meets Dictionary

British Diarist, James Boswell, met Dr. Samuel Johnson for the first time, at Tom Davies's bookstore in London. Boswell was a Scottish advocate (attorney), although he would have preferred a career in literature. Johnsons' 1755 *Dictionary of the English Language* is considered the most significant work of its kind for its precision and wit. He made a tour of Scotland and the Hebrides with Johnson in 1773 and wrote about it in a book published two years later. From 1772 he began assembling materials for the six-volume biography of Johnson that would occupy him for the rest of his life. It was published in 1791. Boswell died in 1795 and Johnson in 1784.

1955: Olga Korbut

The Soviet gymnast was born in Belarus. She was the sweetheart of the 1972 Munich Olympic Games, where she won three gold medals and a silver. She amazed the audience and judges by being the first to somersault backwards on the balance beam. In 1976 Korbut received a team gold medal for the balance beam and was inducted into the Woman's Sports Hall of Fame in 1982.

2003: Sinatra's Post

The Hoboken, New Jersey, USA post office was named for its local boy, Frank Sinatra. Sinatra was born in 1915 and became a teen idol. He evolved into a superstar and Las Vegas draw. He was known as the 'Chairman of the Board' to millions of fans worldwide. His signature songs were *New York, New York, All the Way* and *My Way*. He married four times, made more than 200 albums and appeared in and directed musicals and movies. He died at 82 in Los Angeles in 1998.

1929 The first Academy Awards 'Oscar' ceremony was held in Los Angeles. Recipients were Janet Gaynor and Emil Jennings.

1987 Bobro 400, an enormous barge loaded with 3200 tons of trash, left New York Harbour in search of a dump site. Eight weeks later it returned, after a 9,600 km journey, with the trash still aboard. No other state or country would accept it.

1990 Jim Henson, the *Muppets'* creator, died of pneumonia at age 53.

1990 Sammy Davis Jr., the wiry singer who had performed since age four, died. His signature song was *Candy Man.*

2000 Queen Elizabeth II bestowed the title Dame on English-born veteran actress Elizabeth Taylor.

Sammy Davis, Jr. and Lindsay Wagner.

17 MAY

1918: Eamon De Valera

The Irish national hero was returned to an English prison. The British feared he was collaborating with Germany against them in the peace talks at the end of World War 1. He escaped using a master key smuggled to him in a cake. He fled in disguise to America to raise money from Irish sympathisers for independence from Britain. The Irish Revolutionary Parliament declared its independence and elected de Valera President in his absence. He returned to Ireland in 1920 to find the country in upheaval. He was first imprisoned as a major strategist in the bloody 1916 Easter Rising against the British and had a death sentence commuted to life imprisonment because he had American citizenship. He served several decades as Prime Minister and later as President, struggling to bring unity to the new republic. He died in 1973, age 92.

1961: Eithne Ni Braonáin

The woman we now know as the new age musician, Enya, was born in Donegal, Ireland. One of nine children, she grew up in a musical family. Enya learned saxophone and classical music in her early twenties and began writing songs. Her *Orinoco Flow* was number one on the UK chart in 1988. In 2002 she won the Grammy Award for Best New Age Album for *A Day Without Rain.* Her music was also featured in the movie *The Lord of the Rings* trilogy.

1972: Mia Hamm

Considered to be one of the best all-around woman's soccer players, Hamm was born in Selma, Alabama. At the age of 15 she was the youngest to play on the U.S. National Team, which won two World Cups and two Olympic gold medals. At the 1996 Atlanta Olympics, Hamm was key to the team's winning gold. The Olympic match attracted more spectators to a woman's sporting event than ever before and Mia emerged as a star athlete. Almost overnight, girls across the USA took up the sport. With 158 goals, Hamm holds the international record for scoring.

1749 Physician **Edward Jenner** was born at Berkeley, England. His work with cowpox and smallpox was a milestone in vaccination theory. He died in 1823.

1814 **Norway** became independent from Denmark. It is now a national holiday.

1964 Australia's **Bernard 'Midget' Farrelly** won the first official surfing World Championship at Manly, in Sydney, watched by thousands. Surfing would become one of Australia's most successful international sports.

1971 **Vernie Bennett** of the rock trio Eternal was born in Croydon, England. Eternal includes Easther Bennett and Kelle Bryan. Eternal topped the chart in 1997 with 'I Wanna Be the Only One.'

1975 **Elton John** released the *Captain Fantastic and the Brown Dirt Cowboy* album. It was certified platinum the same day, the first album to do so.

Grammy-award winning song writer and singer Enya.

1927: Grauman's Chinese Theatre

The famous cinema opened on Hollywood Boulevard. The first movie shown was Cecil B. De Mille's *King of Kings*. It was renamed Mann's Chinese Theatre after Ted Mann purchased it in 1973. The theatre is used for movie premieres and attacts millions of visitors each year. Its entranceway immortalises movie star's hands prints, footprints and autographs in cement.

1947: Seabiscuit

The thoroughbred American racehorse died. The undersized, unlikely champion became a symbol of success and hope during the Great Depression. Owner Charles Howard recognised Seabiscuit's potential and bought the horse for just US$8000. Howard, together with trainer Tom Smith and talented jockeys, transformed the 'lazy workhorse' into a top dollar champion. A best-selling book and movie were based on his career.

1980: Mount Saint Helens

The volcano in Oregon erupted unexpectedly at 8.32 a.m. It created a landslide that sheared away the entire northern side of the mountain. At speeds of up to 160 km/h, the debris caused Spirit Lake to flood, which roared down the mountain. Simultaneously, the volcano spewed ash and gases in a mushroom-shaped cloud up to 19 km high. The mountain lost over 500m of its height and a horseshoe-shaped caldera replaced its volcanic cone. By late afternoon the disaster was over. Vegetation was destroyed up to 20km away. Ash settled on Pacific-Northwest cities and spread around the globe.

On May 18, 1980, an earthquake caused a landslide on Mount St. Helens' north face, taking off the top of the mountain and triggering an eruption that killed 57 people, wiped out river valleys and destroyed enough trees to build 300 000 homes.

1804 Napoleon proclaimed himself Emperor of France after a bloodless coup d'etat and was crowned in December.

1897 Frank Capra was born. He was the first to win three Oscars for Best Director.

1964 Chief Kaiser Matanzima, nephew of Nelson Mandela, but a supporter of apartheid, set this as the date for all whites to leave the Transkei, as part of his plan to create a Transkeian Territorial Council. The plans were later rescinded. He died in 2003.

1987 Eavin 'Magic' Johnson won his first basketball Most Valuable Player Award, aged 27. He won again in 1989 and 1990.

1991 Gertrude Elion, co-recipient of the 1988 Nobel Prize in Medicine was the first woman inducted into America's National Inventors Hall of Fame. Her work led to drugs used in treating cancer and in transplants.

19 MAY

1947: David Helfgott

The Australian pianist, whose life-story was portrayed in the movie *Shine*, was born in Melbourne. Helfgott was a child pianist prodigy. After winning several competitions, he had a severe psychiatric breakdown. He was institutionalised on and off for many years. Fellow Aussie, Geoffrey Rush, turned in an Oscar winning performance for his dramatic re-creation of Helfgott's life. After marrying his second wife, Helfgott became more stable and was able to resume performing. He was 1997's top-selling classical artist.

1994: Jackie O

Jacqueline Lee Bouvier Kennedy died at 64 from cancer. She was dubbed the 'Debutante of the Year' in 1947. In 1951 she met 'the most eligible bachelor,' US Senator John Fitzgerald Kennedy. The two had a fairy-tale wedding with 1 300 guests. They had two children, Caroline and John Jr. In 1963 she was at her husband's side when he was assassinated. The images of the widowed Jackie touched the nation's heart. She was criticised for her marriage to the Greek tycoon Aristotle Onassis. Later, she became a book editor. Her strength, charm and impeccable fashion sense endeared Jackie to the American people as one of the finest first ladies.

2002: 'Guboo' Ted Thomas

The last initiated Australian Aboriginal tribal elder, returned to the Dreamtime. Guboo, meaning 'your good friend', was born under a tree in 1909 on the south coast of New South Wales. As a young child, tribal elders instructed him in sacred rituals and ancestral lore and he became the Yuin nation's spiritual leader. He worked at restoring unity between people and with the land. Guboo peacefully fought to protect sacred Aboriginal land. Raising consciousness wherever he went, Guboo taught everyone to thank the Great Spirit for each sunrise and sunset.

1536 Queen Anne (Boleyn) was beheaded for adultery. She was King Henry VIII's second wife.

1910: Halley's Comet The best known comet made its long anticipated return after 75 years, enthralling some viewers and frightening others. It never came closer than 644 000 km from the earth. Cities with few electric lights had particularly good views. US humourist Mark Twain's prophesy came true, 'I came in with it and will go out with it.'

1984 John Betjeman, Britain's popular Poet Laureate died.

1984 Bob Marley's Legend, the compilation album was released on the third anniversary of Marley's death and became an overnight success.

1996 Near Miss: An asteroid came within 452 000 km of Earth.

Jacqueline Lee Bouvier Kennedy Onassis: Debutante of the year, First Lady of the United States, widow, wife of shipping magnate and mother.

20 MAY

1678: Weighing the Mayor

The High Wycombe, Buckinghamshire UK public observes its medieval ritual of the 'weighing in' of the Mayor and his corporation. The first recorded weighing was in 1678, but is believed the practice began much earlier in history. A suspended market scale is used to record the politicians' weight to ensure that no one 'gets fat at the public's expense.' If the weight is the same as the previous year, 'And no more' is said, is greeted by cheers from onlookers. If the politician has gained weight, the announcer states, 'And some more' to jeers.

1799: Honoré de Balzac

The influential French novelist was born in Tours. He failed as a writer until he began writing about realistic, current subjects, such as the French peasants or the French upper class. He wrote at a prodigious rate—at least fifteen printed pages per day. In one year, he wrote 76 novels! *The Human Comedy* portrays more than 2000 characters from every strata of 19th century French society. He made a fortune and formed several famous liaisons with woman, but died in enormous debt in 1850.

1927: Charles Lindbergh

The pioneering pilot left New York in *The Spirit of St. Louis* to fly solo across the Atlantic Ocean in hopes of winning a US$25 000 prize. A reticent man, who was happier in the air alone than on the ground with people, was totally unprepared when the souvenir-seeking mob of 100 000 in France almost destroyed his plane when he landed the next day. His fame brought troubles that plagued him for the rest of his life, including the kidnap-murder of his oldest son. For a time he fled to England to live. Preceding Lindbergh, 66 successful Atlantic flights had been flown, by Zeppelin airships and by the British aviators Alcock and Brown in 1919. However, because Lindbergh flew solo and had movie star looks, he captivated the public.

1944 Singer Joe Cocker was born in Sheffield. One of his enduring classics is 'You Are So Beautiful' which is often sung at weddings.

1978 Mavis Hutchison, 53, arrived in New York City after running across the USA from Coast to Coast in about 69 days. She averaged 45 miles per day.

2000 Leo Blair the son of Tony and Cherie Blair was born. He is the first child born to a serving British Prime Minister in 150 years. He has three brothers and one sister.

2002 East Timor became an independent nation, separate from Indonesia.

2002 Stephen Jay Gould, evolutionary biologist and widely read writer died aged 61.

Xanana Gusmao speaks during a news conference on May 17, 2002 in Dili, East Timor. Gusmao was inaugurated as the first democratically elected president of East Timor.

21 MAY

1804: Pere Lachaise
Paris's hauntingly beautiful and largest cemetery opened. It contains tombs, crypts and final resting places of the famous and the anonymous: all equal in death. Some of the cemetery's most famous dead have unremarkable tombs while other unknowns have the most expensive monuments. With over 100,000 sepulchres the list of famous people buried at Pere Lachaise includes: Abelard and Heloise, Jim Morrison, Oscar Wilde, Sarah Bernhardt, Balzac, Chopin, Marcel Proust, Modigliani and his lover. Karl Marx's daughter is buried there, along with French President Felix Faure, who died in his mistress' arms. There are memorials to mass deaths, such as Nazi concentration camp victims and members of the French Resistance.

1945: Bogey and Bacall
Screen idols, 21-year-old Lauren Bacall and 45-year-old Humphrey Bogart, married in Mansfield, Ohio. They were known as Bogey and Bacall. Bacall is best known for *Key Largo* and dramatic TV work while Bogart is remembered for *The African Queen*, *The Maltese Falcon*, *Casablanca* and *To Have and Have Not*. They had two children together before Bogart died in 1957.

1991: Rajiv Gandhi
The former Indian Prime Minister (1984-89) accepted a bunch of flowers while campaigning for re-election and was assassinated by a bomb hidden in the bouquet. The Gandhi family is sometimes compared to the US Kennedy family for the tragedies that haunt them. Rajiv's mother, the late Prime Minister Indira Gandhi, was assassinated by her Sikh bodyguards in 1984. His only sibling died in an airplane crash. Rajiv's controversial Italian born widow, Sonia, remains active in federal politics.

1471 Albrecht Durer the German engraver and painter was born in Nuremberg.

1881 American National Red Cross was founded in Washington DC by Clara Barton, modelled on the International Red Cross, which had been founded by 16 European countries in 1864.

1909 Sister Maria Innocentia Hummel was born at Massing, Bavaria. Her drawings for kindergarten children were made into figurines. There are Hummel clubs for enthusiasts worldwide.

1927 English actress Kay Kendall best-known for roles such as *The Reluctant Debutante* and *Genevieve* was born. Soon after filming *Once More With Feeling*, Kendall died at 32 from cancer.

1999 Jill Dando: thousands turned out for the funeral of the BBC-TV presenter who was murdered in London.

Married American actors Lauren Bacall and Humphrey Bogart read a movie script together in 1945.

22 MAY

1859: Sir Arthur Conan Doyle

The author, best known for his Sherlock Holmes mysteries, was born in Scotland. While in medical school, he was encouraged by his professor to use careful observation before deduction for the diagnosis of illness. His professor became the model for Doyle's detective Sherlock Holmes. Doyle's stories were so successful that he gave up his medical practice to concentrate on writing. He became irritated at people's obsession with his characters and killed off Holmes in 1894. There was such an outcry he resumed writing about Holmes, Dr. Watson and Baker Street for the next twenty-three years. Doyle is credited with helping to create the literary genre of the detective story. He died in 1930 and is buried at Minstead, Hampshire.

1907: Laurence Olivier

The legendary actor, producer and director was born in Surrey, England. Beginning his career in Birmingham he went on to master most Shakespearian roles. He mesmerised audiences worldwide with his performances in films such as *Rebecca*, *Pride and Prejudice* and *Wuthering Heights*. He appeared in 29 films in thirteen years. With nine Academy Award nominations, three Oscars and five Emmy awards he is considered one of the greatest British actors of all time. He was knighted in 1947 and made Lord Olivier of Brighton in 1970, the first actor to be elevated to the peerage, for his founding directorship of he National Theatre of Great Britain. Olivier died in England in 1989.

1977: Janet Guthrie

A physicist-turned-racing car driver, Guthrie became the first woman driver to qualify for America's Indianapolis 500 race. She had passed the rookie test in 1976 and was also the first woman to drive around the track in actual practice. She did not attempt to qualify because her car was not fast enough. Her No. 27 Lightning-Offenhauser averaged 303.2 kmh to qualify for the 1977 race. She hoped her example would encourage other women to reach for their dreams.

1813 Richard Wagner the German musician and composer was born. His works include *The Ring of Niebelung* and *Tannhauser*.

1924 Charles Aznavour was born in Paris. He is a singer, actor and song-writer. His credits include *Shoot the Piano Player, Candy* and *The Tin Drum*.

1940 Actor Michael Sarrazin was born in Quebec City, Canada. He appeared in *The Flim Flam Man* and *The Reincarnation of Peter Proud*.

1970 Supermodel Naomi Campbell was born in London.

2003 Yuichiro Miura of Japan, aged 70 years and 222 days, became the oldest person to summit Mount Everest.

Japanese mountainer Yuichiro Miura, 70, gives a victory sign in Kathmandu airport, after scaling the 8,848-metre peak.

23 MAY

1873: The Mounties

The Royal Canadian Mounted Police, who work on horseback in often rugged terrain, was formed to track down American fur trappers who murdered First Nation Assiniboines. The idea was based on the Royal Irish Constabulary. Actors Nelson Eddy and Jeanette MacDonald brought the Mounties to prominence in the 1936 smash hit move movie *Rose Marie*.

1949: The Federal Republic of Germany

The FRG, better known as West Germany, was created from the remains of the Nazi dictatorship. Konrad Adenhauer, the visionary statesman, was the Republic's chief architect. He not only fought foreign powers, which had their own blueprints for the new Germany, but he fought internal political battles over a new Constitution. As FRG's first Chancellor, he was in power for fourteen years, saying, 'In politics patience is of major importance and I have a great deal of patience.' Der Alte (The Old Man) who consistently ranks as one of the most admired Germans was Cologne's mayor during the Second World War. He opposed Hitler and was arrested on numerous occasions. Following the War, he challenged the British occupiers who ordered that male civilians salute British officers on the street. He 'could not imagine that the British would want to humiliate a vanquished people in this way.' Adenhauer's most significant accomplishment was the restoration of good relations between Germany, France and Britain after centuries of distrust. He retired in 1963.

2004: Michael Moore goes Gold

The controversial American filmmaker was honoured with the Cannes Film Festival Palme d'Or for *Fahrenheit 9/11*, a scathing attack on George W. Bush's administration. *Fahrenheit 9/11* was the first documentary to receive the award since Jacques Cousteau's *The Silent World*.

1498 Girolamo Savanarola, Florence's powerful ruler, was executed by the Catholic Church.

1926 Joe Slovo, an ally of Nelson Mandela, was born in Lithuania. He was the leader of the South African Communist Party and the first white member of the African National Congress Executive Committee. He died in 1995.

1928 Rosemary Clooney, much-loved singer and aunt to the actor, George, was born on this day.

1933 Joan Collins, TV and movie star was born in London.

1934 Robert Moog, the inventor of the Moog musical synthesiser, was born.

2000: Butrint Albania's World Heritage Site received a major infusion of funding from the World Bank to help preserve its ancient Mediterranean architecture. The 25-square km site includes an ancient city, hills, river and lake: a microcosm of life 3000 years ago.

American director Michael Moore displays his Palme d'Or as he arrives for the official projection of his documentary film *Farenheit 9/11* in Cannes. The film savages US President George W. Bush and examines the period from Bush's 2000 election, through the September 11 attacks and the wars on Afghanistan and Iraq.

24 MAY

1854: New Zealand Parliament

The island nation's parliament sat for the first time. The first capital was in the far north in Auckland. Wellington became the capital in 1865 because of insecurity in Auckland from the Waikato Land Wars. Wellington is in the far south of the North Island and is therefore closer to the South Island.

1941: Robert Alan Zimmerman

Bob Dylan, was born. Dropping out of college, Dylan moved to New York to be with his idol Woody Guthrie who was hospitalised. He became a regular of the club and coffee shop scene. The songwriter quickly became synonymous with the anti-war and civil rights protest movements, writing songs such as *Blowin' in the Wind* and *Mr. Tambourine Man*. Dylan has changed his style over the years reinventing himself with each new album. In 1989 Dylan was inducted into the Rock and Roll Hall of Fame.

2003: Chris Moneymaker

Perhaps because of his last name or even his nickname 'Money,' Moneymaker attracts money like a magnet attracts iron filings. On this day placed a bet of $40 at the 34th Annual World Series of Poker in Las Vegas and won $2.5 million. 'Money' had been playing poker for just three years. For the 2004 Annual World Series, there were 2500 contestants, up from 2003's 800. Each entrant paid a $10 000 entry fee. In 2004 Harrah's Casino has gambled on poker's continued popularity by purchasing the World Series for $30 million.

1870 Jan Christian Smuts, the Dutch Afrikaner was born. He was a revered Boer War guerrilla fighter and drafted the constitution to create the Union of South Africa.

1971 The Australian Liberal Party chose 51-year-old Neville Bonner to fill a vacancy in the Senate. He was the first Aboriginal Senator.

1997 Spice Girls went to the top of the American album chart with *Spice*, the only all female group to top the charts since The Supremes and The Go-Go's.

1999 Susan Lucci's 21-year 'losing' streak ended when the American TV soap opera star of *All My Children* when she received an Emmy Award. She had been very gracious every year.

2001 Pete Townsend received a lifetime achievement award for his services to British music. He composed the rock opera *Tommy* and was an original member of The Who.

Left to right: Emma Bunton, Melanie Chisholm, Victoria Adams, Geri Halliwell and Melanie Brown — The Spice Girls.

25 MAY

1878: Bojangles

The grandson of a slave was born Bill Robinson in Richmond, Virginia, USA. Bojangles is considered one of the greatest tap dancers ever and taught other great tappers—Gene Kelly, Sammy Davis Jr. and Gregory Hines. He died in 1949 in New York City. Jerry Jeff Walker wrote the song *Mr. Bojangles*, which was later recorded by musicians including Bob Dylan, Sammy Davis Jr. and Neil Diamond.

1939: Sir Ian McKellen

The stage and movie actor was born in Burnley, England. The versatile Shakespearean actor won accolades and awards, including a Golden Globe and a Tony for *Amadeus*. McKellen appeared in movies such as *Last Action Hero, Six Degrees of Separation* and *Gods and Monsters*. Most recently, he won the admiration of fans worldwide for his portrayal of Gandolf in *The Lord of the Rings* series. McKellen is active in the Gay Rights movement and played the activist Bill Kraus in *And The Band Played On*. He was knighted by Queen Elizabeth in 1990 and lives with his partner in Limehouse, England.

1981: Dan Goodwin

The 25-year-old daredevil, looking for a challenge and obviously not afraid of heights, donned a Spiderman costume and using suction devices proceeded to climb Sears Tower in Chicago. Climbing the 440 metre, 110-storey Tower took Goodwin six hours. Once he reached the top, police arrested him and charged him with trespassing. He paid his fine and was released.

1997: Elvis Presley

The 'King of Rock and Roll' died US$3 million in debt in 1977, aged 42, but on this day became the world's best-selling posthumous entertainer. His worldwide sales are over one billion records. He has nearly 500 fan clubs, innumerable internet websites and memorabilia collectors.

1963 Funnyman Mike Myers of *Wayne's World, Austin Powers* and *Saturday Night Live*, was born in Scarsborough, Ontario, Canada.

1965 Cassius Clay (Muhammad Ali), in one of the shortest heavyweight fights ever, knocked out challenger Sonny Liston with a 'Phantom punch' in 1 minute and 56 seconds. Many fans were disappointed and demanded refunds.

1977 China lifted its ban on the works of William Shakespeare, which had been banned during the Cultural Revolution for being 'bourgeois.'

1996 Australian Gina G had her first UK hit single with *Ooh Aah Just a Little Bit*.

Love me tender: American rock 'n' roll singer Elvis Presley (1935–1977) with a twelve string guitar.

26 MAY

1940: Dunkirk

Allied soldiers began to be evacuated in one of the most daring manoeuvres in military history. The scale of the evacuation was mind-boggling. Over 200 000 British Expeditionary Force members and 100 000 French and Belgians were transported from Dunkirk, on France's north coast, to safety in England. They had been driven westward by advancing German troops and were apparently hopelessly cornered on the English Channel coast. The evacuation was by every kind of available watercraft—ranging from ferries, to fishing boats, to trawlers and to tiny recreational boats. By 4 June all evacuees had landed in England.

1977: Star Wars

The thrilling science fiction movie was released. One of the most popular and profitable movies ever made, *Star Wars* spawned numerous prequels, sequels and spin-offs, literary adaptations, toys and games. Characters like Luke Skywalker, Darth Vader, Obi-Wan Kenobi, Princess Leia, Yoda and C-3PO have become cultural icons. Written and directed by George Lucas, the series takes place 'A long time ago, in a galaxy far, far away...' The *Star Wars* series are Lucas's attempt at creating modern mythology, drawing on themes from classic literature, of the epic fight between good and evil and empire and democracy.

1998: Sorry Day

Since 1998, 26 May has been recognised in Australia as Sorry Day. It acknowledges 'the Stolen Generation', the forced removal of Aboriginal children from their families throughout the nation as part of a paternalistic, cruel policy. From as early as 1804 until 1969, tens of thousands of children where forced into orphanages and missions, ostensibly to recieve education or training. In fact many were adopted out or used as domestic servants and often abused by their 'caretakers'.

1908 Robert Morley the actor was born. He was often cast as an English gentleman or 'windbag.' He was also known as a brilliant conversationalist.

1954 Egyptian Pharaoh Cheops' funeral ship was found.

1964 Lenny Kravitz multi-talented musician was born in New York.

1966 Actor Helena Bonham Carter was born in London in 1966. She starred in *Room with a View* and *Howard's End*.

2003 Nepali Apa Sherpa's accomplishment in reaching the summit for the 13th time is remarkable, given that one in 10 people who tries to climb Mount Everest dies.

Budjari Aborigine Max Eulo attends an indigenous reconciliation event during the 8th National Sorry Day in Sydney, 26 May 2005. National Sorry Day reflects the human impact of the forcible removal of Aboriginal and Torres Strait Islander children from their families.

27 MAY

1818: Amelia Bloomer

The American reformer and women's rights advocate was born in New York. She focused on the stupidity of women's clothing that restricted women's movements and designed shorter skirts and knee length underwear. Underpants or pantelettes were named after her, first 'Bloomer Costume' and eventually just 'Bloomers.' Amelia Bloomer served as the president of the Iowa Women's Suffrage Association and died in 1894.

1911: Vincent Price

The classic horror actor was born in St. Louis, Missouri. He studied at Yale and then the University of London, where he started acting as a diversion from his studies. After several successful stage performances playing romantic roles, Price's first major film success was in *The House of Usher*. Though he played a variety of roles, he is remembered primarily for his horror films in gothic thrillers, especially works of Edgar Allan Poe. His distinctive low-pitched voice was ideally suited to the 'king of horror films'. Price's last major role was co-starring in the fantasy movie *Edward Scissorhands*. He died in 1993

1964: Jawaharlal Nehru

India's first Prime Minister died in office. Born in 1889 to a wealthy family, Nehru studied law at Cambridge University and served in the Allahabad High Court. Nehru worked with Mohandas Gandhi for over 20 years, to attain India's independence from Great Britain and spent many years in prison. Nehru was elected President of the Indian National Congress in 1929 and played a major role in the creation of two independent nations of India and Pakistan. As Prime Minister he led the country through the rocky period of early independence. His daughter Indira Gandhi succeeded him as Prime Minister.

1703 Peter the Great founded St. Petersburg, Russia, naming it for himself.

1912 Sam Snead 'the winningest' golfer was born in Hot Springs, Virginia.

1931 Paul Kipfer and Auguste Piccard became the first people to reach the stratosphere, over 50 000 feet, in a balloon with a pressurised cabin.

1965 Pat Cash was born in Melbourne. He was a surprise winner at Wimbledon in 1987.

1995 Superman actor Christopher Reeves was thrown from his horse and was paralysed from the neck down. He died on 10 October 2004.

American actor Christopher Reeves during the 1997 Emmy Awards.

28 MAY

1908: Ian Fleming

The journalist and novelist was born in London. A former-intelligence operative, Fleming is best known for his *James Bond* series. He also wrote the children's classic *Chitty Chitty Bang Bang*. He appeared in movies including *Dr. No* and two James Bond movies: *From Russia with Love* and *Goldfinger*. He died in 1964.

2000: People's Walk for Reconciliation

A huge statement by ordinary Australians, the walk went some way towards healing the rift between the Aboriginal and European communities. Hundreds of thousands of people walked across Sydney Harbour Bridge, many carrying signs saying 'Sorry', a word Prime Minister John Howard found impossible to say. A small plane buzzed overhead skywriting the same message. A Corroboree followed at Darling Harbour featuring some of Australia's best-known performers including Jimmy Little, Brendan Gallagher of Karma County, Buzz Bidstrup (GANGgajang) and The Wiggles. Indigenous performers came from as far away as Darwin, Broome and the Torres Strait for this important event.

2003: Beckie Scott

Canada's first Olympic medallist cross-country skier returned from Africa. In contrast to the snowfields where she spends most of her time, she had been a UNICEF Special Representative in Burkina Faso. There, with temperatures at 40-degrees celsius, she toured remote areas to see first-hand the status of UNICEF's programs to promote girls' education. Beckie won a bronze medal at the 2002 Salt Lake City Winter Olympics, by ⅒th second. It was upgraded to silver when a medallist was disqualified. She is also a champion snowboarder and ski sprinter and, in November 2002, received Canada's annual John Semmelink Award for the most outstanding athlete in skiing and snowboarding.

1759 William Pitt was born in Kent. He was British Prime Minister from 1783-1801 and 1804-06, He reduced the huge national debt from the American Revolution. He died in 1806.

1967: Sir Francis Chichester, the British yachtsman returned to Plymouth, England, in his 39-foot sloop *Gypsy Moth* after a nine-month solo circumnavigation of the world. Queen Elizabeth II later knighted Chichester, who had already flown around the world solo, using the same sword Elizabeth 1 had knighted Sir Francis Drake with for his circumnavigation.

1968 Kylie Minogue, singer and actor was born in Melbourne. Her debut album in 1989, *Kylie* sold more than 12 million copies worldwide.

1982 Orient Express, the legendary train resumed running after a long break in service.

1984 Eric Morecambe died age 58 after a long career as one of Britain's most popular comedians. He had just taken six curtain calls at a charity show.

1996 French President Jacques Chirac announced that military conscription would end the next year.

Beckie Scott of Canada receives her bronze medal in the women's cross-country 5 km free pursuit at the medal awards ceremony at the Olympic Medals Plaza during the Salt Lake City Winter Olympic Games in Salt Lake City, Utah.

29 MAY

1953: Mount Everest

After 30 years of attempts by competing nations for the prize of climbing the world's highest mountain, the summit was reached at 11.30 am by New Zealander Edmund Hillary and Tensing Norgay, a Sherpa guide. The expedition had taken years to plan and was executed with military-like precision by Britain's Colonel John Hunt. The news could not have come at a better time for Great Britain, which had suffered mightily during World War II and was still experiencing hardship, some rationing and the recent death of King George VI.

1997: Jeff Buckley

Singer songwriter, Buckley became a cult hero when he drowned at age 30 in the Mississippi River. Whether his drowning was an accident or a suicide is unknown. His one album, *Grace* was released in 1994 to mixed reviews. However, his bittersweet song Hallelujah is widely used in TV shows and in movies. He was very handsome and was voted one of *People Magazine's* '50 Most Beautiful People' in 1995. Buckley's father, Tim, was also a well-known singer-songwriter who died at 28 from a drug overdose.

1998: Barry Goldwater

The Republican elder statesman died aged 89. Born into one of the Arizona Territory's first trading-post families, he was a staunch Conservative and very controversial when he ran for President in 1964 on a platform of heightening US involvement in Vietnam. Later, he became the conscience not only of Conservatism, but of Congress, when he called for Richard Nixon, his own Party leader's impeachment. He also took a stand on homosexuality in the military, saying 'who cares if they shoot blanks, all that matters is that they shoot straight.' He was a skilled aviator who often helped on mercy missions. Because of his family's ties to Arizona's indigenous people, the Hopi Indians bestowed the very rare ceremonial honour on him, by inducting him into their Nation.

1660 King Charles II was restored to the throne after Oliver Cromwell's Commonwealth rule ended. It was also his 30th birthday.

1874 Gilbert K. Chesterton, British essayist was born in London. He wrote five collections of *Father Brown* detective mysteries, plus poems and essays. He died in 1936.

1979 Mary Pickford, actress in more than 100 movies and entrepreneur, 'America's sweetheart' died at age 87. She was born Gladys Louis Smith in Toronto, Canada and was a star from age five.

1982 Pope John Paul II became the first pope to visit UK in 450 years.

1985 Brussels, Belgium: 39 spectators were killed in a rampage at a soccer match.

Mary Pickford (1893–1979) formerly Gladys Mary Smith, the Canadian born silent screen actress who founded United Artists Film Corporation in 1919.

1412: Joan of Arc

'The Maid of Orleans' was born. When she was 12-years-old, she claimed to hear the voices of Saints Michael, Margaret and Catherine telling her to join the French army to fight the invading English. She cut off her hair, to look more like a boy and became an army captain. When the English captured her, a religious tribunal sentenced her to death by fire. She was only 19 when she was burned alive at the stake. In 1920 she was made a saint. Interestingly, when actress Jean Seberg was filming this scene in the movie version of St. Joan's life, her clothing caught on fire.

1960: Boris Pasternak

The Russian-Jewish poet and novelist died, in Moscow, his birthplace. His fame rests on his 1957 novel *Doctor Zhivago*, which portrays the intelligentsia before, during and after the Russian Revolution. He was awarded the Nobel Prize for Literature the next year, but the Soviet Government would not permit him to accept it. *Dr. Zhivago* was not even published in Pasternak's homeland until 1987, long after his death.

1977: TransAlaskan Pipeline

The first oil flowed through the line which runs across Alaska from Prudhoe in the Arctic, to Valdez in the south. It took three weeks for the oil to flow from one end to the other. It was the most expensive private construction project ever undertaken, costing US $7 billion. It faced almost insurmountable obstacles: how to cross 800 rivers, three mountain ranges and how to lay the pipes so that the heat would not melt the permafrost and cause the ground to subside. It has made $130 billion in profits.

1640 Peter Paul Rubens, the 17th century Flemish baroque painter and diplomat, died in Antwerp, Belgium, aged 63.

1744 Alexander Pope, poet, critic and satirist, died age 56 at Twickenham. He was the first English writer to live off his writing earnings. He is famous for *The Rape of the Lock* and *The Dunciad*.

1778 Voltaire French Enlightenment philosopher and writer died in his birthplace, Paris. He fought against religious intolerance and persecution.

1917 John F. Kennedy was born. He was the youngest US president in history, the first Roman Catholic and the first who had seen Naval service. He won a Pulitzer Prize for *Profiles of Courage*.

1972 The world's first National Green Party, the Values Party, was formed in New Zealand at Wellington's Victoria University.

2000 Arsenal Football Club completed the signing of Cameroon International midfielder Bisan Lauren Etame-Mayer from Real Mallorca Club, for £7 million.

John F Kennedy (1917-1963) at age ten.

31 MAY

1813: Blue Mountains Breached

Explorers Gregory Blaxland, William Lawson and William Wentworth arrived at a point in the Blue Mountains from where they could see the vast plains beyond. This was a monumental achievement that opened much-needed farmland for the struggling colony. Governor Macquarie authorised the construction of a road, which was completed within two years, by convict labour.

1942: Sydney Attacked

Three midget Japanese submarines penetrated Sydney Harbour, after two days of reconnaissance, intent on blowing up the US and Australian armada of battleships and cruisers. One became entangled in an anti-sub net and blew itself up. Another fired on the fleet, hitting the *HMAS Kuttabul*, killing 19. This sub eluded capture. The third sub was pursued and the crew committed suicide. The remains of the two submarines were recovered and reconstructed to make a complete sub.

2003: Annular Solar Eclipse

Promising to be one of the most unusual solar eclipses of the 21st century, an annular, or ring eclipse occurs when the Moon's disk is too small to completely cover the Sun's disk, leaving a thin sliver of light around the circumference. Annular eclipses can occur because the Moon's orbit around Earth is not quite a circle. When the Moon is closer to Earth than average, a total solar eclipse can occur. When it is farther than average, an annular eclipse can result.

2004: Civil War Widow

On this day, 139 years after the end of the American Civil War, Alberta Martin, who was thought to be the last Confederate veteran's widow, died, aged 97. The publicity prompted 89-year-old Maudie Hopkins to admit that she married 86-year-old William Cantrell in 1934, when she was just nineteen. Hopkins has outlived three other husbands. The last known Union veteran's widow, Gertrude Janeway died in January 2003.

1809 Fanny Mendelssohn Hensel died in Vienna. A gifted musician and composer, she was very close to her talented brother Felix.

1879 Cornelius Vanderbilt built Madison Square Garden in New York City on the site of the former PT Barnum and Bailey Circus.

1902 The Boer War in Southern Africa ended with the Treaty of Vereeniging. More than 5 000 British and 4 000 Boers died.

1926: Kruger National Park, previously the Sabie Game Reserve in South Africa, was renamed after President Kruger. It borders Mozambique and Zimbabwe and lies between the Limpopo and Crocodile Rivers. It covers about 20 000 square km. It is one of the world's most famous game preserves.

1985 The Football Association banned English clubs from playing in Europe following the deaths of 39 fans at a Heysel, Belgium, game until crowd control was improved.

1999 Geri Halliwell, Ginger of the all girl band, Spice Girls, quit. She went on to a successful solo career, travelled the world as a United Nations ambassador and wrote her autobiography, *If Only.*

Illustration depicting the Australian contingent leaving Sydney for South Africa doing the Boer War campaign.

This page: Crown Prince Dipendra of Nepal at Narayan Hity Royal Palace in Kathmandu. The Crown Prince shot dead 12 members of the Royal Family, including his parents, King Birendra and Queen Aishwarya, Prince Nirajan and Princess Shruti. He then turned the gun on himself.

Opposite: The body of late Queen Aishwarya of Nepal is carried on a Palenquin during her funeral procession in Kathmandu.

1 JUNE

2001: Death in Nepal

Nepal's Crown Prince Dipendra massacred eight members of his family using an assault rifle, as they dined on pizza in the royal palace in Kathmandu. It was a tragedy of Shakespearean proportions involving: regicide, fratricide, matricide, patricide and eventually suicide. In a country where the King is considered a deity, the embodiment of Vishnu, it is hard for Westerners to appreciate the depth of the tragedy. Apparently, Dipendra, fuelled by alcohol, could not accept his parents' decision that if he married the Indian woman he loved, he would have to step aside as heir in favour of his younger brother. His parents wanted him to marry a princess of higher Nepali rank. Dipendra was Eton-educated, known by the nickname 'Dippy', a black-belt karate student and a licensed helicopter pilot. He took his future role as King very seriously and made frequent visits to rural regions to understand Nepali problems. After the shooting, Dipendra lingered on life-support for two days and under the rules of succession ironically was declared King. Kathmandu was placed under martial law after rioting broke out in the grief and turmoil that followed his low-key funeral service. King Birenda's brother became King. Nepal teeters on the brink of civil war, as Maoists continue to recruit in impoverished rural areas.

2004: Australia's Miss Universe

Jennifer Hawkins, a 20-year-old rugby league football cheerleader and model, was crowned Miss Universe in Quito, Ecuador. Born in Newcastle, near Sydney, Hawkins is a willowy blonde who enjoys the outdoors, including surfing and camping. After her reign as Miss Universe, she became a television reporter for an outdoors program.

1937 **Colleen McCullough** author of the best selling *The Thornbirds* was born.
1947 **Jonathan Pryce**, the accomplished stage actor, was born in Wales.
1962 **Samoa** achieved its independence from New Zealand.
1974 **Singer Alanis Morissette** was born in Ottawa, Canada.
1981 **China** published its first English-language newspaper in Peking.
1998 **Ethiopia's Haile Gebrselassie** ran 26:22.75 minutes to set a world record in the 10 000 metres race in Hengelo, Holland.

2 JUNE

1944: Japanese take Anzio, Italy

The 442nd Infantry regiment, all Japanese-Americans, landed in Italy at Naples and soon took Anzio in World War II. Later they were sent to Bruyeres, France and fought the Germans house-to-house. They were the most decorated American unit and suffered an appalling casualty rate. Their slogan was 'Go For Broke,' a term used in playing craps (dice). Partly because of the 442nd's exemplary soldiering, US President Truman ordered the desegregation of the armed forces. One of the 442nd regiment survivors is Hawaii's senior senator, Daniel Inouye, the first Japanese-American congressman, who lost an arm in combat.

1953: Elizabeth Windsor

As a second lieutenant in the World War II's Women's War Services, the young princess drove trucks and repaired vehicles. In contrast, on this day she travelled in a gilded horse-drawn carriage to Westminster Abbey where she was crowned Queen Elizabeth II and officially began her reign as monarch of the British Commonwealth. It was a fairytale occasion with heads of state and the world's monarchs dressed in fine regalia. She addressed the nation by radio to thank them for their good wishes and to publicly thank her husband, Prince Philip, Duke of Edinburgh, for his pledge of loyalty to support her. She was the mother of four-year old Charles and two-year-old Anne. Her reign would see increasing nationalism in the former empire's colonies, with some making the transition peacefully to independence, but others unstable and rocked by civil war.

1965: Steve Waugh

The great cricketer was born in Sydney. In nearly 20 years of Test cricket, he became the most capped player in Test history. He is also Australia's most capped one-day international player with 325 appearances. He and his twin brother Mark played 128 Tests and 244 one-day international, sharing an unbroken partnership of 464 for the fifth wicket for New South Wales against Western Australia in 1990-91. His retirement, at the peak of his career in 2003, took many observers and fans by surprise.

Queen Elizabeth II waving from the balcony of Buckingham Palace with Prince Charles, Princess Margaret and other members of the Royal Family during her coronation ceremonies. Inset: Queen Elizabeth II in her coronation crown. Known as St Edward's Crown, it was made in 1661 for the coronation of King Charles II, and is reputed to contain gold from the crown of Edward the Confessor. It is set with 444 precious stones.

1888 White Australia, the name for a policy that stemmed from inherent racism and a fear of Asian invasion was first used in the Queensland newspaper, *The Boomerang*.

1924 US Congress granted Native Americans citizenship.

1941 Lou Gehrig an American baseball player died of amoyotrophic lateral sclerosis (ALS), which is now often called Gehrigs disease..

1946 Italy became a Republic after King Humbert lost a referendum on monarchy.

1962 Victoria 'Vita' Sackville-West, English writer of the literary Bloomsbury Set, died, age 70. She wrote 13 novels, including *The Edwardians* and a gardening column in *The Observer*.

3 JUNE

1904: Charles Drew

The African-American Olympic athlete and physician was born in Washington, DC. Unable to afford medical school, he became a biology teacher and athletic coach until he was eligible to attend Canada's McGill University Medical School. He became fascinated by blood research and earned a research fellowship at Columbia University, developing techniques for separating plasma and storing blood. He was the first African-American Doctor of Science. During World War II the British invited him to establish a much-needed blood bank. In 1941 he was invited by the American Red Cross to collect blood for the American armed forces. The military at first refused to take African-American blood, causing an uproar. They relented but demanded that blood be separated by race. In 1950 Drew died, from injuries sustained in a car accident in rural Alabama, aged 46.

1924: Quebec's Colleen Dewhurst

The stage actress who had a four-decade career on stage, screen and TV was born. She was one of the greatest interpreters of the work of playwright Eugene O'Neill, debuting on Broadway in *Desire Under the Elms*. She died in 1991 in South Salem, NY.

1992: Land Rights

The High Court of Australia ruled in the trail-blazing Mabo Case that overruled the concept of terra nullius ('unoccupied land'). When Great Britain claimed Australia for the Crown it declared that it did not belong to anyone. Of course, Aborigines had occupied the country for perhaps as long as 60 000 years, longer than Britons had lived in Great Britain. The case was brought by Eddie Mabo of the Meriam people of Murray Island in the Torres Strait. Mabo died in January 1992, just months before the ruling. The Mabo ruling opened the way for Aboriginal tribes to make native title claims for their ancestral lands that had been confiscated. John Howard's Liberal government managed to water down some of the reforms with a 'ten point plan' initiated by the Wik case, giving pastoral landholders more secure tenure and frustrating Aboriginal aspirations to regain freehold title over stolen land.

1924 Franz Kafka the Czechoslovakian novelist and short-story writer died, age 40. His writing explored alienation and self-salvation, such as *The Metamorphosis* and *The Country Doctor*.

1925 Tony Curtis, the film star, was born in New York. He starred in *Some Like It Hot* and *The Defiant Ones*.

1926 Allen Ginsberg, one of the leading Beat generation poets, was born in Newark, New Jersey, USA. He wrote *The Howl*. He died in 1997.

1961 Charles Hart, composer and lyricist, was born in London.

1987 Andres Segovia, virtuoso classical guitarist, died, aged 94. He was born in Spain.

Poet Allen Ginsberg speaks on the 'Charlie Rose' show in 1994, in New York City.

4 JUNE

1738: King George III

The king who 'lost the American Colonies' was born in London and reigned from 1760-1820. He tried to extract taxes from the colonies to pay large debts incurred for wars against the French and in India. King George 'flew into a rage' when the 'insolent' colonists refused to pay the taxes, which led to the American Revolution. George III is also remembered as 'the mad king' because he inherited porphyria, a disease which also afflicted Mary Queen of Scots. He suffered his first attack in 1765, four years after his marriage to Queen Charlotte, and became progressively insane and blind. He spent his time in isolation, often in straight jackets and behind bars, in Windsor Castle, until his death at the age of 82 in 1820.

1940: We Shall Never Surrender

Winston Churchill, the Prime Minister of Great Britain, gave his famous World War II speech, boosting the nation's morale in face of an expected Nazi invasion. The speech was delivered to welcome the 'miracle of deliverance' as some 338 000 stranded troops were rescued from Dunkirk. Churchill told the world that 'We shall fight on the beaches . . . we shall never surrender'.

1989: Tiananmen Square Massacre

The Chinese army brutally crushed pro-democracy protests in Tiananmen Square, Beijing, China. Tanks rumbled through the capital as soldiers shot unarmed protesters in cold blood. Later they fired on crowds of residents who were attempting to help the wounded or identify loved ones. Troops entered Beijing's university campus beating and killing those they suspected of involvement in the protests. More were arrested and later executed or imprisoned. An estimated 7000 perished, though the true figure will never be known. Demonstrators, mainly students, had occupied the square for seven weeks, asking for democratic reforms. The ferocity of the attack took many by surprise and brought condemnation from around the world. Australia's Prime Minister, Bob Hawke, openly wept at a televised press conference and offered refuge to Chinese students studying in Australia.

1966 Cecilia Bartolli, a mezzo-soprano diva (opera singer), was born in Rome.

1970 Tonga was granted its independence from Britain. It is a national holiday.

1975 Angelina Jolie, the film star, was born in Los Angeles. She starred in *Alexander* and won an Oscar for *Girl, Interrupted*. She is a UNICEF Ambassador.

2003: The American Film Institute (AFI) unveiled their list of the top 100 movie heroes and villains of all time. The favourites included

Atticus Finch: the greatest hero in *To Kill a Mockingbird*. Gregory Peck gave the finest performance of his illustrious career in this courtroom drama.

Indiana Jones: the second greatest movie hero was Jones in *Raiders of the Lost Ark*. Harrison Ford played the role.

Hannibal Lecter: the evil cannibal was voted the worst villain in *Silence of the Lambs*. Sir Anthony Hopkins gave a spine-chilling performance.

Norman Bates: the villain in Arthur Hitchcock's *Psycho* took second place. Anthony Perkins played the role so convincingly that Janet Leigh never showered again!

Sir Winston Churchill was a controversial Tory politician with a chequered career. When he replaced Neville Chamberlain as British Prime Minister, in the darkest days of World War II, his inspiring speeches and 'never say die' attitude stiffened the resolve of the isolated island nation.

5 JUNE

1932: Christy Brown

Born with severe cerebral palsy in Dublin, Brown was the tenth of twenty-two children. He could not eat, drink, or dress without assistance. He was thought incapable of movement and communication for his first five years. Using his left foot, he taught himself to write with chalk on the floor. When he was 21, his autobiography was published to critical acclaim. The movie that earned Daniel Day-Lewis an Academy Award for Best Actor, *My Left Foot,* was based on his remarkable story. Books of verse and books about life in the Irish slums followed. Brown was a keen observer of himself, his thoughts and the literary process. He married when he was 40. He died at age 49 from asphyxiation.

1963: The Profumo Affair

The British Secretary of War, John Profumo, resigned after revealing that he had an intimate relationship with an alleged prostitute, Christine Keeler. In March, Profumo had categorically denied any relationship with Keeler, who was also involved with Captain Eugene Ivanov, a naval attaché to the Russian Embassy in London. Concerns were expressed in Parliament that Keeler may have passed sensitive nuclear secrets to Ivanov. Profumo retaliated by threatening to sue for slander and libel. After Keeler disappeared to avoid testifying, Profumo resigned, admitting that he had lied. On June 8, Dr Stephen Ward, who had introduced the couple, was arrested and later committed suicide. There was speculation that he had been scapegoat. Keeler was later sentenced to nine months in prison. An inquiry concluded that although national security had not been compromised, the government should have acted more promptly. The scandal brought down Harold MacMillan's Conservative government and Labour's Harold Wilson came to power the next year.

1988: Kay Cottee

The thirty-four-year-old Australian, arrived in Sydney Harbour—the first woman to sail around the world solo, non-stop and unassisted. It had taken 139 days. Her arrival coincided with Australia's bicentennial year and she was named Australian of the Year. She had been born with a hole in her heart, which made her prone to fatigue, but she battled huge waves and almost being run down by a fishing vessel to accomplish her feat. Her boat was the 12-metre Cavalier sloop *Blackmore's First Lady*.

1870 Jeannie Taylor was born. Known by her married name, Mrs Aeneas Gunn, she wrote *We of the Never Never* about her experiences with Central Australian Aborigines.

1900 Dennis Gabor was born in Budapest, Hungary, which he left in 1933 to live in the UK. He won the Nobel Prize in 1971 for his work in holography.

1928 Charles Kingsford Smith landed *the Southern Cross* in Fiji six days after leaving the US Pacific coast. This was the longest sea flight to date.

1939 Margaret Drabble, the writer, was born in 1939, is known for her contemporary novels such as *The Peppered Moth*.

1980 Gulf and Western, an American manufacturer, announced the development of a battery suitable for running an electric car.

1977 Apple released its new computer, the fully assembled Apple II. It was open to third party plug ins and its 4Kb memory was considered huge at the time.

Apple co-founder Steve Jobs posing with an Apple II computer.

6 JUNE

1937: Neeme Jarvi

Widely hailed as one of the greatest living conductors, Jarvi was born into the musical Jarvi dynasty in Tallinn, Estonia. For 15 years he has conducted both the Detroit Symphony Orchestra and Sweden's Gothenburg Symphony. His children are all professional musicians. His son, Paavo, is Music Director of the Cincinnati Symphony Orchestra. His daughter Maarika, is a freelance flutist. His third son, Kristjan, is a founder and conductor of Absolute Ensemble and conductor of an Austrian orchestra.

1944: D-Day

Taking advantage of poor weather, the Allied forces made a surprise landing in German-held Normandy, France. Operation Overlord, known to history as D-Day, involved an incredible fleet of 2700 ships, two million tons of material, 50 000 tanks, plus jeeps and trucks. Twelve Allied nations provided over three million troops led by Britain's Field Marshall Bernard Law Montgomery, or 'Monty', and Allied Commander, America's General 'Ike' Eisenhower, who instructed the parachutists to acheive, 'Full victory-nothing else.' Residents of the village of Saint Mere Eglise woke at sunrise to see wave after wave of parachutists floating down from the sky like a dream come true. Despite heavy German fire, over 150 000 Allies landed by nightfall at Utah Beach and Omaha Beach. The second front had at last opened.

1999: Tony Lockett

The legendary full forward of the Sydney Swans Australian Football League (AFL) broke a 62-year-old record. The record of 1299 career goals had been held by Gordon Coventry. Lockett kicked nine goals in a match against Victoria's Collingwood, Coventry's former club, and went on to finish the day with 1306 goals in 265 games. In 1996 he thrilled the crowd when he kicked a point after the siren to defeat Victoria's Essendon Club. This put the Swans into their first AFL grand final since they moved to Sydney in 1981, in a move to broaden the game's appeal from its Victorian base.

1799 Alexander Pushkin, Russia's 'Shakespeare' was born, best known for using everyday language in his works. He died in a duel in 1837.

1903 Aram Khachaturian was born in Armenia and is known for his lively compositions based on its folk music and dances.

1925 Both Munich and Berlin held 50th birthday celebrations for the great writer and Nobel Laureate Thomas Mann. He wrote *The Magic Mountain* and *Death in Venice*.

1933 The first 'drive-in' movie theatre opened in Camden, New Jersey.

1956 Bjorn Borg, Swedish tennis player, was born. He was the youngest player to win the British Open at 18-years-of-age in 1974.

1968 Robert 'Bobby' F. Kennedy, a candidate for the US Presidency, was assassinated. The younger brother of the assassinated John F. Kennedy, he had been shot the previous day.

American senator Robert F Kennedy (1925-1968) speaking at an outdoor rally during his campaign for US president in 1968. He was assassinated just as he clinched the vital California primary and looked set to win the Democratic nomination as presidential candidate.

7 JUNE

1946: Bill Kreutzmann Jr

The co-founder of the Grateful Dead, drummer and singer, was born. With Jerry Garcia as front man, Bob Weir, Bill Sommers and Vince Welnick and later Mickey Hart, the acid rock band attracted a worldwide following of fans known as 'Deadheads' for 30 years. Their last concert was just one month before Garcia's death in 1995, age 53. Some of the fans' favourites were 'Box of Rain', 'Truckin' Candyman' and 'Not Fade Away'.

1958: Prince

The musician and singer, also known as 'His Royal Baldness,' was born in Minneapolis, Minnesota. His birth name was Prince Rogers Nelson. He had an unstable childhood, but was surrounded with music and attended a James Brown concert when he was 10, which made him determined to be a musician. He learned drums, bass, piano and saxophone. His first success with his smooth falsetto voice was 1999. Problems with a recording contract led him to change his name to a symbol that was unpronounceable. He was often called 'The Artist Previously Known as Prince.' Among his best known songs are 'When Doves Cry' and his best known album is *Purple Rain*. In 2000 he re-adopted his name.

1970: E M Forster

The British writer died age 91. He wrote *Where Angels Fear to Tread, Howard's End, A Room with a View* and *A Passage to India*. The last two explored the joys and tensions that ensued when different cultures collided. His brother and father died when he was an infant and he was extremely frail. His doting mother and attentive aunts called him the 'Important One.' His schooling was cruel, but he in contrast was sensitive to the joys and delights of life, which made him both an acute observer and a fine writer.

1778 Fashion leader Beau Brummel was born in London, but his sarcasm led to poverty.

1939 King George VI and his wife, Elizabeth, (later known as the Queen Mother) was the first monarch to visit the USA.

1940 Singer Tom Jones was born in Pontypridd, Wales. His signature songs include *It's Not Unusual* and *What's New Pussycat?*

1945 Eleanor Roosevelt, quite possibly the most remarkable First Lady in American history, addressed the plight of migrant farm workers in her widely read *'My Day'* newspaper column.

1952 Actor Liam Neeson was born in Northern Ireland, and is best known for *Schindler's List, Ethan Frome* and *Les Miserables.*

Actor Liam Neeson arrives at the 68th annual Drama League Annual Awards Luncheon May 10, 2002 in New York City. Proceeds from the luncheon support the Drama League Project, a training program for emerging directors.

8 JUNE

1964: Hendrik Verwoerd

South Africa's Prime Minister announced 'the 90-day detention' provision would be suspended in January 1965. There had been intense protest by university professors and opposition members when it was extended for a year. Verwoerd was a Nazi sympathiser and the architect of South Africa's strict apartheid laws. During the War, he criticised the UK for giving refuge to Jews. Verwoerd was assassinated two years later, stabbed to death by a messenger on the floor of Parliament. Ironically the assassin said Verwoerd was 'helping blacks to the detriment of whites. Johannes Vorster succeeded him as Prime Minister, but protests and violence continued to escalate.

2000: Olympic Flame

After starting its journey in Athens, in May the Olympic Flame arrived in Sydney, Australia. It travelled through twelve Asian nations and was flown to central Australia's sacred Uluru Aboriginal site. Kunmanare 'Reggie' Uluru accepted the torch from Governor General Sir William Deane. Uluru said, 'We are all very happy the firestick has come to my father's place and we welcome you to our country. We have been using traditional firesticks since ancient times and we are proud to welcome this special torch here today.' Eight members of Uluru's family passed the torch to Australia's first Aboriginal Olympic gold medallist, Nova Peris-Kneebone, running barefoot in reverence for the land. Peris-Kneebone won gold for field hockey in the 1996 Games. She was the first of 11 000 runners in the 99-day, 27 000km relay around Australia.

2004: Prince Louis XVII of France

The heart of the young prince was finally buried after 200 years of various resting places, including sitting on a shelf. The Prince spent three years in solitary confinement before succumbing to tuberculosis. A doctor, performing an autopsy on the 10-year-old son of King Louis XVI and Marie Antoinette, secretly removed Prince Louis XVII's royal heart from his body in 1795, according to custom. The heart of the little heir to the French throne was finally entombed with his parents, who were executed in the Revolution. It was rumoured that perhaps he had survived, but DNA tests confirmed that it was his heart.

793 Vikings on English soil: the first recorded raid occurred at Lindisfarne Island, or Holy Island, off the north-east coast, near the Scottish border. It is a tidal island and now a Nature Reserve.

1783 Iceland's Laki volcano erupted violently, spewing lava for eight months causing famine and the deaths of about 10 000 people. Its acid rain and haze reached Europe.

1887 Herman Hollerith, American statistician received a patent for a punch card calculator. It was used in US and UK Census. His firm later merged with IBM.

1950 Sir Thomas Blamey became the only Field Marshal in Australian history. It is a rank above 'General.' One of the few remaining Marshals is Philip, the Duke of Edinburgh. Prince Charles declined the title.

1970 Abraham Maslow Jewish/Russian/ American psychologist died, age 62. He is best known for his *Hierarchy of Human Needs*, whose pinnacle is 'self actualisation.'

Sir William Deane, Governor General of Australia, delivers an address during the Olympic Lighting Ceremony in Ancient Olympia, Greece. Deane was a speaker of great compassion and well loved as Governor General.

9 JUNE

1803: Captain Matthew Flinders

Flinders returned to Port Jackson, Sydney, after his successful circumnavigation of Australia in the *Investigator*. He ranks second to Captain James Cook among explorers of his time. He joined the Royal Navy at age 15 and sailed with William Bligh to Tahiti in 1791. He arrived in New South Wales in 1794 and with naval surgeon, George Bass, explored the Sydney region's coast and charted the coastline of Queensland and Tasmania. Flinders returned to England and married, but three months later the Admiralty sent him to chart the whole Australian coastline. On his return voyage to England he was imprisoned by the French in Mauritius for six years. The two countries were at war. Flinders worked on his journals, but his health was ruined. He published his *Voyage to Terra Australis* the day before his death in 1814.

1961: Michael J Fox

The Canadian actor was born in Edmonton, but raised in Vancouver. He enjoyed enormous popularity in TV series, such as *Family Ties* and *Spin City* and in movie series such as *Back to the Future*. He was able to use his youthful looks and slight stature to play far younger roles. Fox revealed in 1998 that, although he looked really young, he had contracted an old people's disease, Parkinson's. It is a serious neurological condition and Fox had brain surgery to ease the symptoms. He is very active in the Parkinson's Action Network.

1963: Johnny Depp

Now a resident of France, Depp was born on this day. After a leading role in a teen TV series, *21 Jump Street*, he went from obscurity to overnight success. He had originally dropped out of school, which he hated, to be a guitarist with his band. *The Kids* had some success, until they moved to Hollywood, where there was too much competition. He accepted an offer to work in television and gradually moved up to roles that suited his talent, such as *Edward Scissorhands*. A major box office draw, Depp disdains what he perceives to be Hollywood's shallowness and excess. Depp's movies include *Pirates of the Caribbean*, *Don Juan de Marcos* and *The Shooter*.

1934 Donald Duck was 'born'. His 'father' was the great animator, Walt Disney.

1958 England's Gatwick Airport was opened after extensions and modernising that cost seven million pounds.

1964 William 'Max' Aitken, Lord Beaverbrook, the Canadian/British politician and business magnate died. He was such a specialist in making deals, that HG Wells predicted God would be kept busy with 'Max' trying to merge Heaven and Hell.

1970 Jordan's King Hussein narrowly escaped an assassination attempt.

1975 The first live broadcast was made by radio from the British House of Commons.

Walt Disney with some of his creations, including Donald Duck, Pluto, Goofy, Pinocchio, Bambi, Mickey Mouse, Snow White and Dopey.

10 JUNE

1921: Duke of Edinburgh

Prince Philip was born into the Greek royal family on Corfu as Philip Schelswig-Holstein-Sonderburg-Glucksberg. Anti-monarchy activists had threatened his destitute family with death and Great Britain's King George V sent a naval vessel to their rescue. His father abandoned the family to live with his mistress and his mother had a breakdown. Young Philip was shuttled from family to family, until he became a ward of Lord Louis Mountbatten. Philip served with distinction in the navy and it is believed that Mountbatten played matchmaker to Philip and Elizabeth. When Elizabeth became Queen, Philip assumed the role of Consort. He served as patron to more than 800 organisations and was the first president of the World Wildlife Fund. He has a special interest in athletics and established the Duke of Edinburgh Awards for skills and leadership. A love of science and technology made him keenly aware of the importance of radio and television. He was the first royal interviewed on television, in 1961.

1972: Marcus Nicholls

The most famous of the legendary Wellington, New Zealand, rugby family, died age 71. He is described as a 'complete rugby craftsman.' His goal kicking was superb. For nine years from 1921, he played for the All Blacks in 51 matches, including 10 internationals. He was the top points scorer for the famed 1924 'Invincibles', scoring 103 points. Nicholls' father and son also played for Wellington. Two brothers, Harold and Harry played for New Zealand.

2000: Millennium Bridge

London's new pedestrian bridge was closed for review and repair, two days after opening, because it swayed excessively, making people seasick. The link over the River Thames was tested and designed to cope with a degree of movement, but when crowds walked on 'The Wobbly Bridge' they compensated for the movement by walking in synchronisation, which exacerbated the wobble. Some engineers claimed that 'people were walking the wrong way' which gave the press a field day. Dampers costing £5 million were installed on the £18 million bridge and it reopened two years later.

1928 Maurice Sendak, the American children's book illustrator was born. His classic work is *Where the Wild Things Are.*

1931 When Arturo Toscanini refused to play the Italian Fascist anthem, he and his wife were beaten outside a theatre, his passport was confiscated and he was put under house arrest for a month. After student demonstrations won his release, he left Italy.

1934 Frederick Delius the German/English composer died. He was 72. He wrote chamber works and operas. His work includes *On Hearing the First Cuckoo in Spring* and *Romeo and Juliet.*

1967 Israel ends the six-day war. Israeli forces stop their advance into Syria and comply with a UN ceasefire bringing to an end six days of fighting on three fronts. They retain the Palestinian lands occupied during this conflict despite numerous United Nations resolutions demanding their withdrawal.

1976 Adolph Zukor, who founded Paramount Theatres, died, aged 103.

1982 Rainer Werner Fassbinder, German movie director died, aged 36. He wrote, produced and directed about fifty movies, including *Querelle.*

Some of the 2000 volunteers who walked across the Millennium Bridge during a stress test of London's newest bridge. The bridge was closed three days after it opened due to a persistent 'wobble' in the structure when people used it. A series of 90 shock absorbers were fitted to the 350-m suspension bridge, which links London's financial centre and the South Bank of the River Thames.

11 JUNE

1910: Jacques Yves Cousteau

The famed underwater explorer was born in France. A sickly child, he took up swimming and became fascinated by the mysteries of the deep. As a teen he published his first book about a trip to Mexico and bought his first movie camera. During World War II he lived near the Mediterranean and experimented with underwater cameras and goggles. Wanting to increase the length of time spent underwater, in 1943, with Emil Gagnan, he invented the Aqualung and then the Self-Contained Underwater Breathing Apparatus (SCUBA) using compressed air. In 1950 Cousteau bought the ship *Calypso* and began exploring and taking photos and filming. He made 80 documentaries, won two Oscars and introduced millions to the wonders of the sea.

1939: Jackie Stewart

The charming Scottish racing car driver was born. In a short career of 18 years he won 27 Grand Prix races and was world champion three times. Wearing a tartan-patterned racing helmet, he was nicknamed the 'Flying Scot.' In his late twenties, during three years on the training Formula Three circuit, he won an impressive 11 of his 13 races. In 1965 he had an experience that changed his life. He crashed and emergency rescue services were so inadequate that even the ambulance drivers were lost. Stewart realised that had his injuries been worse, he would have died. He retired in 1973, age 34, after 100 races. He is remembered for making Formula One racing a safer sport and for his Grand Prix wins record that stood for two decades.

1961: Hovercraft

Inventor Sir Christopher Cockerel's first full-sized hovercraft, the Saunders-Roe Nautical One (SRN1), was launched. Engineers had tried various methods of using air to reduce the drag on ships, but it was not until 1952 that the British inventor devised a practical vehicle. Cockerel experimented with a vacuum cleaner motor and two cylindrical cans, showing that a vehicle could be mobile by riding on an air cushion over water or mud. Cockerell added a jet system to retain the air cushion under the vehicle. During the 1960s hovercraft were rapidly developed worldwide and became increasingly sophisticated and larger. They were used on the English Channel until the Chunnel opened.

1776 John Constable, the landscape painter, was born in Suffolk, UK. The area is known as 'Constable Country.' His work went unappreciated during his lifetime and he only sold twenty paintings.

1892 The Limelight Dept., one of the world's first and most productive movie studios officially began operating Melbourne, Australia. It was owned by the Salvation Army and produced more than 300 evangelical movies in its nineteen years of operation.

1955 Le Mans, France: more than eighty spectators died and about 100 were injured when two racing cars collided. The cars then spun into the crowded grandstand.

1998 Dame Catherine Cookson died, age 91. She was England's most widely read novelist, writing under several pseudonyms, including Katie McMullen and Catherine Marchant.

2002 The West Bank, Palestine. Israel began construction of a controversial 360-km barrier to separate Israeli settlements from areas inhabited by Palestinians.

The Saunders Roe SRN-1, the first full sized working hovercraft, on display at Cowes, Isle of Wight.

12 JUNE

1886: A.B. 'Banjo' Paterson

The Australian bush poet's first poem was published on this day, when he was 22-years-old. He was a successful attorney, but adventure always called. Paterson's first poetry collection, *The Man from Snowy River*, was published in 1895. It sold out within a week and was published another four times in six months. It continues to be the best-selling Australian volume of poetry. It was made into a movie in 1982. Paterson's poetry helped his countrymen develop a sense of their national identity. Never one to stay still, after a few years farming, he became a war correspondent in first the Boer War and then World War 1. He also wrote children's books, dozens of radio plays and novels. He wrote the words to the song Waltzing Matilda, about a shearer, that is an unofficial national anthem. He said Australians have three basic rights, 'Life, liberty and the pursuit of horse racing.'

2002: Sir Paul Marries Again

Heather Mills and Sir Paul McCartney were married at an ancient church in Ireland. Because they had announced their engagement in India, they served Indian food at their reception. Mills indicated in early 2005 that she sometimes wished she had not met McCartney as she enjoyed her previous life without the constant media scrutiny. Mills is much admired for overcoming adversity in her life. Her mother abandoned her at age nine and she was responsible for her siblings. She became a successful model, which led to a goodwill trip to Croatia. Seeing the horrors of war there she campaigned for victims of landmines in Croatia. In 1993 she had a traumatic accident with a police motorcycle and a partial leg amputation. She became an increasingly outspoken advocate against landmines and for the supply of prosthetic devices. She has helped more than 27 000 people acquire prostheses. She wrote an autobiography *Out on a Limb* nine years ago, which has been re-released as *A Single Step*.

1839 Baseball celebrated its 100th anniversary by dedicating its Hall of Fame in Cooperstown, New York.

1964 In South Africa's infamous Rivonia Trial, eight of the eleven African National Congress leaders were sentenced to life imprisonment.

1977 A three-week hostage siege in the Netherlands ended when the military seized a train in which more than fifty passengers were held and a nearby school where four children were held hostage.

1982 In the largest anti-nuclear weapons demonstration in American history, 800 000 marchers assembled in New York City.

2001 Collins Concise English Dictionary released an updated version that included words like multi-tasking, spamming and reality TV.

Australian bush poet, adventure man and war journalist, Banjo Patterson is a legend and remembered for his 'Man from Snowy River' poem and 'Waltzing Matilda' song, which are defining icons for Australians.

13 JUNE

1935: Christo

The artist, known for wrapping large man-made and natural features in fabric, was born in Bulgaria. *Running Fence* is a 24-mile long, 18-foot high white fabric fence in California. He draped the Gap at South Head, Sydney. He wrapped Germany's Reichstag in silver cloth and blue rope and set up a field of umbrellas in Japan and California. For his latest installation, *The Gates*, with his wife Jeanne-Claude, in New York's Central Park, 7 500 saffron-coloured banners are situated along every path, like standing domino pieces. Hundreds of thousands of New Yorkers visited the display in February 2005, with mixed reactions. Christo's works are unique, ephemeral, surreal and bold.

1981: Shane Gould

The Australian Olympian was invested as a Member of the Order of the British Empire for services to swimming. In a brief three-year career she held every women's freestyle record from 100 metres to 1500 metres. She was the first woman to break the 17-minute mark for the 1500 metres. At age 15 she won five medals, including three gold, at the 1972 Olympic Games in Munich and was named Australian of the Year. In 1974 she was voted the world's all-time best woman freestyle swimmer. She retired from competitive swimming at 16 and at age 19, she married and moved to Western Australia.

2001: frENZy

The Royal New Zealand Ballet first performed frENZy: a tribute to the rock band Split Enz, New Zealand's most celebrated rock band. The ballet included a forty person Maori kapa haka group, Matare I Orehu and dancers wearing silver tutus, pointed shoes and zoot suits to bring the band's humour and eccentricities to life. Split Enz's hits, from 1972 to when they broke up in 1984, include Six Months in a Leaky Boat, Message to My Girl and I Got You. The band formed in 1971, when brothers Tim and Neil Finn joined Phil Judd, Geoff and Mike Chunn, Robert Gillies, Eddie Rayner and Noel Crombie.

1886 King Ludwig of Bavaria, known as Ludwig the Mad, died mysteriously age 21. He was certainly eccentric and possibly insane. He built the Neuschwanstein fairy tale castle.
1931 Mohandas Gandhi announced that on his next visit to London to discuss India's independence, he would live in a garret with the English poor, with whom he identified.
1951 Labor's Joseph Chifley, Australia's 16th Prime Minister, died. A former engine driver, he identified with the common man and won many benefits for them. He introduced post-war immigration policies and social security.
1980 Walter Rodney, Prominent Guyanese activist and scholar was murdered. He earned his doctorate in London. He increased political awareness throughout the Caribbean nations.
2004 A four kilogram meteorite crashed through the roof of Brenda and Phil Archer's home near Auckland, New Zealand. The roof and some furniture were destroyed.

The Gates art installation in a snowy Central Park, New York City. Created by Christo and Jeanne-Claude, *The Gates* featured 7500 frames with hanging orange-tinted fabric, creating what the artists billed as 'a visual golden river' along 37 km of footpaths in the park.

1942: New Zealand 'Invaded'

The American invasion of New Zealand began when 5000 American Marines landed in Wellington. Their arrival was described in the press as a 'miracle.' New Zealand's troops were fighting in Greece and the Middle East when Pearl Harbour was attacked by the Japanese in 1941. Three days later, two British naval ships were sunk in the Pacific and Singapore was about to fall. Suddenly New Zealand seemed defenceless and feared the worst. At best the Kiwis could recruit a volunteer force of youths and veterans to patrol the coast. Residents dug backyard air raid shelters and installed blackout windows. In March 1942 American President Roosevelt agreed to help New Zealand if it left its troops in the Middle East. The two-month wait for the Americans to arrive was agonisingly long. When the first American echelon came steaming into Wellington Harbour without warning, crowds of grateful Kiwis rushed to meet them. Eventually more than 100 000 would be rotated through New Zealand.

1961: Boy George

The flamboyant singer was born in Kent, England. He formed the band Culture Club, in 1981 and was its lead singer. He was as much known for his compositions, such as 'Karma Chameleon', 'Tense Nervous Headache' and 'Boyfriend' as for his androgyny, flamboyant makeup and dress and drug use. His first major American success came in the 1990s with his rendition of the Crying Game for the movie by the same name. He also achieved success as a DJ.

1961: Hard Rock

The first Hard Rock Café (HRC) opened in London. Two Americans, Isaac Tigrett and Peter Morton, chose a former car showroom at Piccadilly Circus for the café, which featured inexpensive food and rock and roll memorabilia on the walls. The first major gift was from Eric Clapton, who liked hanging out there. In the early 1980s, Morton opened HRC in four American cities, while Tigrett opened five in the USA, Paris and Berlin. Both partners eventually sold their shares to bigger corporations, who have further expanded the HRC concept to over 36 countries. Fans in the 1980s enjoyed collecting T-shirts from HRC locations worldwide; now the current fad is to collect as many pins as possible.

1381 England's King Richard II met John ball, Jack Straw and Wat Tyler, the leaders of the Essex and Kent Peasants' Revolt against the third poll tax.

1822 Mathematician Charles Babbage presented a paper to the Royal Astronomical Society on a Difference Engine, a preliminary step towards creating a computer. The paper was titled 'Note on the application of machinery to the computation of astronomical and mathematical tables'.

1933 Jerzy Kosinski the Polish novelist was born. He wrote *The Painted Bird* about a Gypsy child's harrowing experiences in the Second World War. He died in 1999.

1940 An ill-prepared Paris fell to the Nazi invaders in the Second World War.

1950 Rowan Williams The Anglican Archbishop of Canterbury was born in Swansea, Wales. He was enthroned in 2003. He attended Pope John Paul II's funeral, the first Archbishop of Canterbury to attend a papal funeral since King Henry VIII's reign.

The first Hard Rock Cafe in London, England.

15 JUNE

1892: Sir Keith Park

The Kiwi behind the Battle of Britain, was born in Thames and educated in Dunedin. He fought in World War 1 as a distinguished fighter pilot on the Western Front. The 6 foot 5 inch giant, sometimes barely fitted into a plane seat! During the Second World War, he was in charge of air protection in 1940 for the retreating Allies from Dunkirk, intercepting the Luftwaffe. He was the last to leave the Dunkirk skies. When the Germans launched their barrage on London, known as the Battle of Britain later that same year, Park was in charge of the Royal Air Force (RAF). He was a fine leader under pressure, who used calm judgment using a new radar system to track the thousands of Luftwaffe planes and to deploy RAF fighter planes. If needed, he would fly reconnaissance missions. He was next placed in charge of what looked like a hopeless mission-to defend Malta. Instead of taking the defence, he took the offense and once again succeeded. Park was knighted, not once, but twice!

1964: Margaret Laurence

Margaret Laurence's publisher Knopf released her novel, *A Jest of God*, a short story collection and an African memoir-all. Laurence was born in a small prairie town near Winnipeg and began writing as soon as she could read. She spent extended periods of time overseas in England and Africa. She is considered one of Canada's finest authors, helping to shape the post-Second World War consciousness. Alcoholism, cancer and personal tragedy led to her suicide in 1987. She is remembered for *The Stone Angel*, *The Fire-Dwellers* and *The Diviners*.

2002: Sir Mick

Queen Elizabeth II knighted Rolling Stones' Mick Jagger in her Queen Jubilee Birthday Honours. Jagger's 4-year-old son Gabriel thought it meant his father would go to a castle to see a king and wear armour. For four decades Jagger has been known as a wild rock and roller and very anti-establishment, constantly making headlines for drug abuse and his behaviour. Tony Blair, who would have helped with the knighthood recommendations, is known to have always admired 'Old Rubber Lips' Jagger. Some other honourees were Trevor Nunn, artistic director of the Royal National Theatre, Dr. Jonathan Miller, known for directing plays and operas and as a cast member of the Beyond the Fringe quartet and Harold Pinter, playwright of *The Birthday Party* and *The Caretaker*.

1667 Dr. Jean Baptiste directed the first fully documented blood transfusion, transfusing sheep blood to a teenager. When the youth died, Baptiste was charged with murder.

1909 International Cricket Conference (now Council). Representatives from England, Australia and South Africa met determine the rules of the game. In 1926, India, New Zealand and the West Indies were added to the ICC. There are now ten nations.

1925 One in three American women now drives. Brunettes are better drivers than blondes, reports the National Taxicab Owners Association.

1956 Ted Hughes and Sylvia Plath, both acclaimed poets, married. Hughes became a British Poet Laureate.

1977 Spain held its first free election in 41 years and elected a centrist-right coalition led by Adolfo Suarez, who had been appointed Prime Minister the previous year by King Juan Carlos.

Lead singer for the Rolling Stones, Sir Mick Jagger, smiles after receiving his knighthood at Buckingham Palace, London. He joins pop knights Sir Paul McCartney and Sir Elton John.

16 JUNE

1936: Dr. Charles Perkins

The trailblazing Aboriginal football (soccer) player, activist and public servant was born at the Old Telegraph Station, Northern Territory. He moved to Adelaide as a teenager where he stood out as a soccer player. At 21, a Hungarian soccer club recruited him and he became one of their highest paid players. On his return to Australia he played soccer in both Adelaide and Sydney. His earnings made his goal of a university degree realistic and he became the first Aboriginal male university graduate in 1966. In 1965, he was one of the leaders of a Freedom Ride through rural New South Wales to end segregation. Perkins held prestigious positions in the Aboriginal civil rights movement, including Aboriginal Development Commission chair. As the Secretary of the Deptartment of Aboriginal Affairs, he was the first Aborigine to head a federal department. He also founded the Aboriginal Cricket Association and initiated their 1988 UK tour. Perkins died aged 64, in 2000.

1960: Psycho

The suspenseful movie directed by Sir Alfred Hitchcock opened in New York. Anthony Perkins played Norman Bates, a quiet, withdrawn motel manager who was apparently fixated on his mother. Janet Leigh played the part of Marion Crane, a thief who thought she had succeeded in stealing $40 000 of her boss' money to finance a new life with her boyfriend. Hitchcock was afraid of heights, open spaces, uniforms and birds. He probed these anxieties and phobias in his movies, of which Psycho would be his scariest, and one of the most frightening ever made. Hitchcock started making movies in England in the silent era. His first, *The Lodger* was based on the infamous Jack the Ripper case. He moved to Hollywood and produced a string of classics: *Rebecca* (for which he won an Oscar) *Rear Window, The Birds* and *North by North-West*, and the *Alfred Hitchcock Presents* TV series.

Museum goers look at displays in the Hector Peterson museum, opened in 2002 in Soweto, South Africa. Peterson was killed during the student uprising in Soweto in 1976. Black school students demonstrated against the Afrikaans language imposed on them by the Apartheid government. The museum opened on Youth Day.

1487 The Battle of Stoke Field is considered by historians to mark the end of the English War of the Roses.

1871 The University Test Act permitted students to attend Oxford, Cambridge and Durham Universities without religious tests, unless the field of study was theology.

1948 First airplane skyjacking occurred when a Cathay Pacific seaplane was taken over.

1977 Werner Von Braun, the East Prussian born rocket scientist died, age 65. He developed the V-2 bomb that blitzed Great Britain during the Second World War. When he was captured by America, he became a leader in the American civilian space program.

1977 Leonid Brezhnev became USSR president. His term was a time of economic stagnation, persecution of dissidents and invasion of Afghanistan and Czechoslovakia. He died in 1982.

17 JUNE

1972: Watergate

One of America's most damaging political scandals began in Washington, DC. Employees of the Republican Party's Committee to Re-elect the President broke into the Democratic Party Headquarters in the Watergate Hotel. It was an act of political espionage, to see their opponents' files and lists of contributors. Investigations by police and *Washington Post* journalists, Bob Woodward and Carl Bernstein, implicated the White House and Republican President Richard M. Nixon. After lengthy inquiries and hearings, the threat of impeachment forced Nixon to resign in August. Since then suspected political impropriety is often dubbed –gate: Reagan's Iran-gate, Clinton's Whitewater-gate, South Africa's Propaganda-gate and New Zealand's picture-gate.

1980: Venus Williams

The formidable tennis player, Venus Ebone Starr Williams, was born. Fifteen months later, her sister Serena was born. Venus was the first African-America woman to win singles and doubles titles at Wimbledon, the US Open and Olympic medals in the same year, 2000. Her five-year sponsorship with Reebok was the richest endorsement ever for a female athlete. Serena has won seven Grand Slams. Both have been ranked Number 1 player in the world. At the Australian Open Venus and Serena were the first two African-American sisters to compete in any professional event. Serena was the first African-American to win the US Open since 1958.

2003: Frane Selak

Croatia's, if not the world's, unluckiest man, finally had Lady Luck shine on him. He survived seven major accidents, including: a train derailment into a frozen river in 1962, a plane crash, several car accidents and a bus that plunged into another river. There were fatalities in all of these accidents. Two of his cars exploded into flames and Selak was run over by a bus. When the former music teacher purchased his first ever ticket in the Croatia national lottery, he won £600 000. He said he felt his 'life was just beginning.' The 74 year old planned to buy a house, a car and marry his 54 year old girlfriend.

1703 John Wesley was born in Epworth, England. He and his brother Charles founded Methodism, which started as a nickname for their 'methodical' habits. The Methodists became known for their evangelical preaching.

1898 Maurits Cornelis (MC) Escher was born in Leeuwarden in the Netherlands. His art explored infinity and used tricks of perception and perspective, for example *Ascending and Descending* with lines of people in an infinite loop. He died in 1972.

1931 Italian leader Benito Mussolini said that religion was indispensable, but that the state had priority and 'That's me.'

1932 Chilean Socialist Republic leaders Marmaduke Grove and Eduardo Matte were exiled to Easter Island, ending the Republican form of government.

1944 Independence granted to Iceland by Denmark. It is now a national holiday.

American President Richard Nixon sits in the Oval Office of the White House in Washington DC during the Watergate scandal that led to his impeachment and resignation.

18 JUNE

1815: The Battle of Waterloo

Napoleon 'met his Waterloo' when he was defeated by combined British/Prussian troops under the command of the Duke of Wellington, Arthur Wellesley and Gebhart Leberecht von Blücher. The battle began well for the well-equipped French. Napoleon drove a wedge between the Prussian and British forces, leading to a Prussian defeat and a British retreat to Waterloo, a village in central Belgium. Napoleon caught up with them, but rain prevented his moving his cannons into position. After ten hours of fighting, the Prussians joined the British and turned the tide. Napoleon retreated to Paris, abdicated and surrendered. If Napoleon had won, world history would have been different. He might have re-established his Empire and made France the dominant European power. Instead, Britain emerged as the world's super power for a century.

1886: George Leigh Mallory

The adventurer who tried three times to climb Mount Everest was born in Cheshire, England. He was Britain's best climber. On his second attempt an avalanche swept seven Sherpas away and he was forced to retreat only 2000 feet from the summit. He was last seen on 8 June 1924, with his climbing partner Andrew 'Sandy' Irvine, approaching the difficult Second Step of Everest's North Face. In 1933 Irvine's ice axe and a body was found. Mallory's mummified body was found in 1999, but not near any of the conventional routes. Did they reach the summit and die on the way down? Climbers are hoping that his camera will be found. Asked what was the appeal of trying to climb Everest, Mallory famously replied, 'Because it is there.'

1942: Paul McCartney

Sir Paul McCartney was born in Liverpool. McCartney is one of two surviving Beatles. Beatlemania began in England, but quickly spread around the world and 'I Want to Hold Your Hand' topped the American charts in 1964. They were a mouthpiece for the generation, preaching love, peace and fun. When the Beatles split in 1970, McCartney formed Wings with his late wife Linda. A self-taught musician McCartney composed 'A Liverpool Oratorio' in homage to his birthplace. He is married to Heather Mills.

After 75 years buried in ice, George Leigh Mallory's petrified body was found in May 1999, during an unusual spring thaw. Mallaroy dissapeared in 1924 with fellow climber Andrew Irvine, while attempting to reach the summit of Mount Everest.

1685 James Scott, the first Duke of Monmouth, declared himself King of England, in what is called the Monmouth Rebellion.

1902 Samuel Butler, English satirist died, age 67. He was best known for *Erehwon*, which is 'nowhere' spelled backwards.

1942 Hans Vonk Dutch conductor was born. He conducted the esteemed Royal Concertgebouw and the St. Louis Symphony. He died aged 62 after a long illness.

1945 William Joyce, known as Lord Haw-Haw, was charged with treason for broadcasting fascist propaganda to Great Britain during World War II. He was American/Irish, but because he travelled on a British passport, the charge went through and he was executed the following year.

1949 Chris van Allsberg, children's book writer and illustrator was born in Michigan, USA. His very successful *Polar Express* was made into a movie in 2004, with Tom Hanks.

19 JUNE

1885: Statue of Liberty

One of the world's most recognisable statues, a gift from France, arrived in USA. French sculptor Edouard Laboulaye designed the giant 50 metre statue, which was shipped in two hundred packing cases and took 15-months to assemble. Six years later, the chief immigrant entry station was opened nearby at Ellis Island. For the next 32 years, more than 12 million immigrants arriving in New York Harbour were welcomed to their new homeland by the sight of Lady Liberty.

1940: Niagara Sunk

Germany made several sorties into the Pacific Ocean during the Second World War. Mines were laid off New Zealand and on this day, the *RMS Niagara*, a Trans-Pacific passenger ship on the New Zealand to Hawaii run, struck a mine north of Auckland. All 349 passengers and crew were rescued, but the ship sank in 200 metres of water. More than $5 million of gold bullion owned by the Bank of England sank with the ship. The gold was to purchase American weapons for the Battle of Britain. Salvage operations commenced immediately and the wreck was located the next year. Ninety-four percent of the gold was recovered within 12-months. Other operations have since recovered more.

1948: Nick Drake

The singer and songwriter was born in Burma. He later moved to the UK and at times lived in Europe. He was overwhelmed by shyness and was sometimes too incapacitated to perform. His debut album, *Five Leaves Left* was released in 1969, while a student at Cambridge University. The melancholic songs have exquisite guitar playing. He moved to London and recorded his classic *Bryter Layter* with several musicians including John Cale and Richard Thompson. It was more jazzy and positive than his previous works and included one of his best-known songs, 'Northern Sky'. When the album failed to sell in quantity he fell into depression and committed suicide aged 26.

1928 Barry Took, British comedian was born in London. He was the BBC's presenter of *Points of View* and *The News.*

1978 Garfield, the lasagna loving comic strip cat, was 'born.' He was created by Jim Davis.

1987 Guns N' Roses, the heavy metal band made their debut at London's Marquee Club.

1993 Sir William Golding, Nobel laureate, died. He wrote allegorical novels about the clash of barbarism and reason, such as *The Lord of the Flies* and *Pincher Martin.* He was born in Newquay, Cornwall in 1911.

1999 Prince Edward, third son of Queen Elizabeth II and Philip, Duke of Edinburgh, married Sophie Rhys-Jones. They are the Earl and Duchess of Wessex.

The Statue Of Liberty during construction in Paris. Designed by the French sculptor Frederick Bartholdi, the statue was presented to the United States by France in 1876. The right arm can be seen in the forground.

20 JUNE

1893: Axe Murders

The verdict was announced in Elizabeth 'Lizzy' Borden's murder trial. She was charged with hacking her wealthy father and stepmother to death in their home in Fall River, Massachusetts. Cheers and applause erupted in the crowded courthouse when the jury foreman read a verdict of 'not guilty.' The 33-year-old demure Christian probably did commit the murders, but the prosecution failed to convince the jury. A children's skipping rhyme indicts her:
Lizzy Borden took an axe – gave her mother forty whacks
When she saw what she had done – she gave her father forty-one.

1985: Avril Lavigne

The young Canadian superstar was born in Napanee, Ontario. At the age of two she decided to be a rock star and by her early teens was writing songs and composing music. At 16 she was 'discovered' and moved to New York. It was still not what she wanted, so Lavigne moved to Los Angeles and released her debut album, *Under My Skin*, in 2002 with the help of Clif Magness the producer/songwriter. It sold 15 million copies. On her birthday in 2004 Avril won the MuchMusic Video Award in the People's Choice Award category of Best Canadian Artists.

1967: Nicole Kidman

The actress was born in Honolulu, Hawaii to Australian parents, began her stage career at age 10 and performed in low budget Australian movies at age 14. Kidman first received critical acclaim at 19 for her performance in *Dead Calm*. She has starred in *Portrait of a Lady, Moulin Rouge* and *Eyes Wide Shut*. Since her much-publicised divorce from Tom Cruise she been cast in roles that allow her to explore her versatility. She won an Oscar for her portrayal of Virginia Woolf in *The Hours*. Australia calls her 'Our Nicole' with pride. She earned a place in Guinness World Records for earning the highest fee ever paid to an actor for a TV advertisement for Chanel Number 5 perfume in 2003. She earned US$928 800 per minute for the four-minute spot. Her fellow-countryman, Baz Luhrmann conceived and directed the advertisement. Kidman is Australia's richest woman under 40 years of age, well ahead of Elle Macpherson and Kylie Minogue.

1898 The Spanish commander of Guam did not know the Spanish-American war was in progress and had no ammunition. He was forced to surrender to the captain of the USS Charleston and Guam remains an American occupied territory.

1925 Herr Schaetzle demonstrated his wireless telephone for automobiles.

1928 Raoul Amundsen Norwegian polar explorer died when his seaplane crashed near Spitzbergen. He was attempting to rescue the crew of a downed dirigible.

1940 Actor John Mahoney was born in Manchester, England. He stars as Frasier's father in the sitcom *Frasier*.

1960 Nan Winton became the first woman reader of the national news on BBC TV.

Canadian singer Avril Lavigne on stage in Frankfurt, Germany during her 2005 European tour.

21 JUNE

1967: Albert John Lutuli

The distinguished South African civil rights leader died age 69. He spent decades as an educator and religious activist. A man of noble bearing and adamant in his demands for justice and equality, Lutuli was forced by apartheid proponent, Prime Minister Verwoerd, to choose between his chieftainship of his Kholwa people and leadership of the African National Congress (ANC). Lutuli saw no option and endured insults by the press and politicians who called him 'ex-chief Lutuli.' When the champion for non-violent change was awarded the 1960 Nobel Peace Prize, Prime Minister John Vorster scornfully stated, 'The government fully realises that the award was not made on merit.' Hard of hearing in his final years, Lutuli was killed crossing a train track in his home village.

1982: Prince William

Princess Diana gave birth to her first son, second in line to the British throne, after his father, Charles, the Prince of Wales. He was the first heir to the throne born in a hospital, not in a palace. His brother Harry was born two years later. With his good looks, athleticism and royal heritage Prince William is one of the world's most 'eligible bachelors.'

2003: Harry Potter

J K Rowling's *Harry Potter and the Order of the Phoenix* was released. At 8.5 million copies it was the biggest first-run release of any book in history. It is the fifth in the Harry Potter series about the child wizard. Joanne Rowling was born in Chipping Sodbury, England in 1965 and always planned on being a writer. Her first book was written under her initials, to appeal to both boys and girls, since boys are often reluctant to read books by female authors. She succeeded in encouraging boys to read, no mean feat, as her books run about 400-pages. Her books are also popular with adults for their humour, satire and fantasy.

1940 Canadian Northwest Passage: The first successful west to east navigation began at Vancouver, British Columbia.
1948 Peter Goldmark of CBS Laboratories developed the first long playing (LP) record.
1965 The Byrds, a folk-rock band released their first album, the hugely successful *Mr. Tambourine Man*.
1996 National Aboriginal Day was proclaimed in Canada to honour Canada's diversity and the contributions of the First Nations, Inuit and Metis.
2001 Billy Collins was proclaimed as the next Poet Laureate of the USA.

Harry Potter board games on display, along with books from the Potter series. The sixth book, *Harry Potter and the Half-Blood Prince* was released in July 2005.

1969: Judy Garland

Forever associated with the role of Dorothy in the 1939 classic *The Wizard of Oz*, Garland died age 47 in London. She was born Frances Gumm at Grand Rapids, Minnesota. She went from a family stage act to a movie career at age 13 and appeared in Andy Hardy movies with Mickey Rooney in some 1940s smash hit musicals. Alongside her short career as a singer and a movie star, she had a tragic and turbulent private life, with five marriages and psychiatric problems. She never achieved the happiness she sang about in her trademark song, 'Somewhere Over the Rainbow'.

1998: Whacky Collections

US News and World Report featured some favourite off beat American museums including: *Barney Smith's Toilet Seat Art Museum* in San Antonio, Texas. Smith dressed up 458 discarded seats with deer antlers, feathers and Boy Scout badges. In Leroy, NY is a museum featuring the colourful wiggly, gelatin dessert known as Jell-O. The Museum includes paintings and even a device called the jellometer, used to measure Jell-O density. Finally, in Washington DC is the *Squished Penny Museum*. The co-curator Petey More has a collection of 250 souvenir pennies from amusement parks.

2004: Mattie Stepanek

The boy who inspired millions of Americans died age 13. Stepanek was born with a rare form of muscular dystrophy, which killed his three older siblings in infancy. His mother has the adult onset form. Wise beyond his years, Stepanek said, 'Life is so fragile and so temporary that we shouldn't waste time fighting. It's easy to care about people we know personally. What's sometimes difficult is to care for people we don't know about.' Knowing that he would not reach 20, he had three wishes: publishing a book, meeting Oprah Winfrey and befriending former American President Jimmy Carter. He achieved his goals and was much loved by both Winfrey and Carter. Stepanek published *Heartsongs* his first poetry volume, when he was 11. Carter, himself a poet, wrote the forward to Stepanek's second volume, *Journey Through Heartsongs*. He was a frequent guest on Winfrey's show and she gave his eulogy. Stepanek's tenacity to live amazed his doctors. When he died America mourned a special angel.

1633 Galileo Galilei was placed under house arrest, until his death in 1642. Church authorities felt threatened by his telescope observations and theories about Earth's and the Sun's orbits.

1894 The first major automobile race was held, with cars making a round-trip from Paris to Rouen, France.

1938 African-American Joe Louis knocked out the champion Germany's Max Schmeling just 124 seconds into the World heavyweight fight. Schmeling was not a Nazi, but newspapers exploited the victory as democracy wins over fascism. When Schmeling died in 2004, it was revealed he had helped Louis financially and even paid for his funeral.

1980 Australia's first test-tube baby and world's fourth, born in Melbourne.

1987 Fred Astaire, the ultimate dancer, died age 88. Partnered with Ginger Rogers he performed in movies such as *Shall We Dance* and *Top Hat*.

American actor Judy Garland (1922–1969), known to millions of children as Dorothy, holding Toto, the dog for the film, *The Wizard Of Oz*, directed by Victor Fleming.

23 JUNE

1947: Bryan Brown

The laconic Australian actor was born in Sydney. Once an insurance salesman, he has a long and distinguished acting career. With his rugged yet handsome features, he plays the typical Aussie 'bloke.' Among his memorable roles are the lead in the television series *A Town Like Alice,* and roles in *Gallipoli, Breaker Morant, Gorillas in the Mist, Along Came Polly* and *The Odd Angry Shot.* He is married to English actor and director Rachel Ward. Both recieved Member of the Order of Australia awards in 2005 for their services to the community, raising awareness of social justice and work with charitable organisations.

1987: Slava

American President Ronald Reagan presented Mstislav 'Slava' Rostropovovich with the Medal of Freedom. Rostropovovich, the world's greatest cellist, has received ninety major awards from twenty-five countries, and forty honourary degrees. His mother liked to joke that her longer than usual pregnancy gave him his beautiful hands that contribute to his cello playing. After studying with Prokofiev and Shostakovich, the teenager became an overnight celebrity when he won the first-ever USSR contest for young musicians in 1945. For a quarter of a century he was one of the USSR's most inspiring performers, conductors and composers receiving his nation's highest award, the Lenin Prize. Rostropovovich and his wife, the famed opera singer Galina Vishnevskaya, were stripped of their Soviet citizenship and exiled for their outspoken support for the dissident writer Alexander Solzhenitsyn in 1974. He was appointed music director of the American National Symphony, a post he held for 17 years. In 1989 he played at the opening of the Berlin Wall. Rostropovovich's Russian citizenship was restored in 1990 on his triumphal return.

2003: Penguins Crossing

The City of Cape Town, South Africa, erected probably the world's first 'Penguins Crossing' signs on Simon's Town main road to reduce penguin fatalities. The flightless birds cross the roads in search of suitable nesting areas during the breeding season.

1919 Estonia celebrated its victory over Germany in World War 1. It is a national holiday.
1921 Luxembourg's Royal Highness, Grand Duke Jean was born. It is a national holiday that also celebrates its independence as a principality in 963.
1922 When Walter Hagen won the British Open golf tournament; he was the first American-born winner to do so. He won three more times in the 1920s.
1940 Wilma Rudolph became the first female Olympian to win three gold medals at one Games. She won the 100-m, 200-m and 400-m sprints at Rome in 1960.
2004 Extreme Mongolia race, two Kiwis John O'Loghlen and Rosa Volz were the first Non Mongolians across the finishing line in this 100km race.

Bryan Brown and wife Rachel Ward, pictured at the premiere of *Dear Claudia* in February 1999 in Sydney, Australia. They were named Members of the Order of Australia in June 2005 for their continuing contributions to social awareness, charities and services to the community.

24 JUNE

1880: Horace A. Ford

Regarded as Britain's greatest archer, Ford died on this day. Ford studied 'the Queen of Sports' intensively and published his analysis in *Archery: Its Theory and Practice*. By codifying the sport, Ford helped established rules and principles of style. No longer a 'bows and arrows' game, it became a serious sport. He first competed in 1845; four years later he won the national championship, which he did for the next consecutive decade. His record score stood for an incredible 72 years. Ford was an imposing figure on the field, for his strength, nerve and his stature (two metres). After a five-year injury break, he won his 12th Grand National Championship in 1867.

1930: Sir Charles Kingsford Smith

Nicknamed 'Smithy', the Australian was the first aviator to circumnavigate the world, landing at his starting point, Oakland, California. Born in Victoria in 1897 he took up flying as a young man. In his first major triumph he flew around Australia in ten and a half days in 1927, halving the previous record. Smith and his unlicensed co-pilot, Charles Ulm, had several brushes with death. Once they crashed in the remote Kimberley area in Western Australian, surviving on brandy and coffee for 10 days. Smithy was a popular hero and was mobbed by crowds whenever he landed. A grateful New Zealand gave him a prize of £2000 in 1928, when he flew from Sydney to Christchurch in 14 hours, compared to the four-day boat trip. Smithy and Ulm flew blind in the open two cockpit monoplane for eight-hours in a violent hail and windstorm. When the radio failed the navigator used a long pole to pass messages to Smithy. Despite his feats, Smith had a fear of flying over water after nearly drowning as a child. At age 38, his plane disappeared over the Bay of Bengal in 1935. Sydney's international airport is named in his honour.

1314 The Battle of Bannockburn is celebrated throughout Scotland. It is the anniversary of Scottish independence with Robert the Bruce's victory over England.

1622 Macau the Portuguese defeated the Dutch who wanted to take over the colony in China. It is a day of celebration and homage to Macau's patron Saint, Saint John the Baptist. Like Hong Kong, Macau has now reverted to Chinese administration.

1699 Bevis Marks Synagogue. Construction began on the oldest synagogue in London.

1899 Australia played its first international rugby contest against Britain in Sydney. They won 13-3. They dubbed themselves The Wallabies in 1909.

1976 An anonymous gift of $1.2 million enabled the purchase of the site of the famous Battle of Hastings of 1066.

Robert Bruce (1274 - 1329), King of Scots from 1306, in combat against Sir Henry de Bohun before the Battle of Bannockburn in 1314.

25 JUNE

1846: Cook's Tour

Thomas Cook led his first organised Scottish travel tour from his Leicester office. The group contained 350 'excursionists,' on a five-day railway jaunt. The first stop was Glasgow, where they heard a speech on 'The Natural, Moral and Political Effects of Temperance.' In Edinburgh there were more speeches, but the rest of the time was a holiday. The previous year Cook led trips to Wales and launched his European excursions in 1855 with a group of 50 tourists to Belgium, Germany and France. A good time was had by all, but Cook lost money. His company survives and a long, circuitous journey is still called a 'Cook's Tour.'

1950: The Korean War

The first major test of the United Nations' solidarity began when North Korea invaded South Korea. The Communist North faced little resistance as they marched toward the capital, Seoul. America, South Korea's ally, was taken by surprise. Despite reassurances from the American Ambassador that there was no war, the United Nations' Security Council met in emergency session and issued a sharply worded memorandum demanding the immediate withdrawal of the North's troops. Seoul fell on June 28th and on 30 June, President Truman authorised the use of American troops in concert with the United Nations after Soviet reassurance that it would not interfere. Australia, the UK, Canada, France and India all supported the South with material or military support. China assisted the North. General Douglas MacArthur promised to have the troops home by Christmas 1950 but was later relieved of his command for publicly criticising the President's foreign policy priorities. The war ended in 1953, after millions of civilians and soldiers had died. It is often called the *Forgotten War*, overshadowed by World War II and Vietnam.

1876 Colonel George Custer and more than 200 men were killed at *the Battle of the Little Bighorn* in Montana when they attacked a lightly defended camp of Sioux Indians. Chief Sitting Bull ambushed and killed Custer's entire force in the biggest victory by Indians against the Americans.

1926 The first Miss Australia contest was held. Its winner was Western Australia's Beryl Mills.

1942 Sir Peter Blake the UK contemporary pop artist was born.

1968 Bobby Bonds of the San Francisco Giants baseball team won a grand slam in his first league game, the first player to do so.

1991 Croatia and Slovenia The two Yugoslavian republics formally seceded from Yugoslavia. Forty-eight hours later, Yugoslavia invaded Slovenia.

Main picture: George Armstrong Custer (1839-1876) with an advance unit of the Seventh US Cavalry, discovered a Sioux camp and launched an immediate attack. Chief Sitting Bull had hidden the bulk of the Sioux and Cheyenne warriors, who surrounded and wiped out Custer's entire force of 250 men.

Inset: Chief Tatanka Yotaka or Sitting Bull of the Sioux in 1881. He became head of the Strong Heart warrior society in 1856 and chief of the entire Sioux nation in 1867. Sitting Bull led the Sioux resistance against settlers before touring America as part of Buffalo Bill's Wild West Show.

26 JUNE

1892: Pearl Buck

The writer was born in West Virginia but lived in China with her missionary parents until she was 32, except for time spent at school and college in America. In 1929 she wrote her Pulitzer Prize winning novel, *The Good Earth*, the story of a peasant who survived famine, betrayal and dishonour to become a wealthy landowner. She also wrote biographies of her parents, *The Exile* and *Fighting Angel: Portrait of a Soul*. Buck wrote dozens of other novels about the confrontation between East and West. Buck helped Westerners gain an insight into everyday life and customs of her adopted country. She won the Nobel Prize for Literature in 1938. Later she established an adoption centre for Asian-American children. She died in 1973 in Vermont, aged 74.

1959: St Lawrence Seaway

Queen Elizabeth II, Canada's Prime Minister John Diefenbaker and American President Dwight D. Eisenhower dedicated the St. Lawrence Seaway in Quebec, Canada. The enormous Seaway along the 1930-km-long St. Lawrence River connected the Atlantic Ocean with the Great Lakes. Seven locks were constructed in the joint American-Canadian project to raise giant ships by an elevation of 70m.

2000: Human Genome Project

In a joint announcement with British Prime Minister Tony Blair, American President Clinton stated, 'Without a doubt, this is the most important, most wondrous map ever produced by humankind.' Blair said that it would open up possibilities for scientists to fight disease at its basic genetic roots.' Two teams of scientists competed on the project. One was taxpayer funded: the Human Genome Project, led by Dr. Francis Collins and one venture capital funded: Celera Genomics, led by Dr. J. Craig Venter, who was perceived as a maverick. When he discovered sequencing techniques that shortened the time for the project by 10 years, he was rebuffed by Collins' team. In a face-saving gesture and for the 'good of scientific research' they appeared together at the announcement. Clinton said, 'In genetic terms, all human beings are more than 99.9 per cent the same.'

1541 Francesco Pizarro the Spanish conqueror of Peru died in Lima, Peru.

1929 The American Ambassador to the Court of St. James's, Charles G. Dawes, broke with tradition in choosing not to wear traditional silk breeches to a Buckingham Palace reception. He was the only one attending to not do so. He wore long trousers and tailcoat.

1963 American President John F. Kennedy, to thundering applause, proclaimed to the Berlin crowd, "Ich bin ein Berliner."

1974 Bar Coded: In Troy, Ohio, USA, a packet of chewing gum with a UPC was scanned. It was the first time a bar code was used.

1980 Richard Thorp the Australian born architect won a design contest for a new Parliament House in Canberra. Work began the next year.

The Australian Eureka flag flies over Canberra's most prominent land mark, Parliament House, cleverly disguised as a grassy knoll.

27 JUNE

1826: James Smithson

The English scientist James Smithson died. Although he never visited the USA, he left his enormous wealth for a museum. His will stated 'to found at Washington under the name of the Smithsonian Institution, (an) establishment for the increase and diffusion of knowledge among men.' Smithson was born in Paris, the illegitimate son of Hugh Smithson (the first Duke of Northumberland) and Elizabeth Keate Hungerford Macie in about 1765. He inherited a considerable estate from his mother's family. He travelled widely in Europe, conducting research in chemistry, mineralogy and geology. Unfortunately, the bulk of his personal papers and documents were destroyed by fire in 1865. The Smithsonian is today an important American museum.

1880: Helen Keller

One of the most extraordinary people of the 20th century was born in Alabama. A childhood illness left her deaf and blind at 18 months old. All she could remember from her sighted days were shadows of moving trees on her bedroom wall. She learned English, German and Greek and learned to sing. Extraordinarily intelligent, she graduated with honours from Radcliffe College. She was a Socialist, who loved horseback riding and waltzing and had a distinguished career as an author and lecturer.

1999: Mr Skateboard

Tony Hawk executed a perfect 900 at the X Games. It was the first time anyone had accomplished the skateboarding feat. Hawk had practiced for 13 years to accomplish it. The 900 involves two and a half airborne rotations. Skateboarding made Hawk a legend and wealthy. He retired after the 900, at 31. Hawk had been skateboarding since he was nine years old, progressing from street skating to vertical (vert), learning to become airborne off an empty swimming pool lip, long before there were skateboard parks. Hawk got his first sponsor, Dogtown Skateboards at age 12 in 1980 and he turned professional at 14. He won 73 and placed second in 19 of the 103 pro contests he entered. The annual X Games feature gravity defying, heart-stopping skills, like the 'Ollie' named after Alan Gelfand. Skateboarders were once outlawed from mainstream society, but their skill and lightning reflexes are increasingly recognised.

1844 Joseph Smith Jr. the founding prophet of the Mormon Church, the Church of Jesus of Latter Day Saints was murdered. Smith was a candidate for the American presidency and the first to be assassinated.

1846 Charles Stewart Parnell, the Irish nationalist was born in County Wicklow, Ireland. His political career was destroyed when he had an affair with another politician's wife. In 1891 they married, he lost an election and he died.

1927 American Marines adopted a new mascot—the English bulldog.

1929 The first colour television—with an image the size of a postage stamp—was demonstrated at Bell Labs in New York. The images tested were the Union Jack, an American Flag and a rose bouquet.

1991 When Thurgood Marshall, the high profile African-American Associate Justice resigned from the American Supreme Court, it was the end of a liberal Court. A conservative, Clarence Thomas, replaced him.

Champion skateboarder, American Tony Hawk, flips in the air as he rides the half pipe in the skateboard competition during the 1998 X Games.

28 JUNE

1712: Jean-Jacques Rousseau

The influential philosopher was born. He was one of the Enlightenment thinkers, along with writers Voltaire, Denis Diderot, Johannes von Goethe, Dr. Samuel Johnson, William Blake, musicians, Wolfgang Amadeus Mozart and Joseph Haydn, economist Adam Smith and philosophers Immanuel Kant and Rousseau. In a time of war, heavy taxation and oppressive government in Europe, the Enlightenment thinkers were heavily influenced by the events in North America, where the colonists were prepared to fight against England's oppressive government. This served as an example to France, whose own Revolution was brewing. Eventually the winds of enlightenment, logic and reason swept across Europe. Rousseau made the statement in *The Social Contract* in 1762 'Man is born free and everywhere he is in chains.'

1880: Ned Kelly

Australia's favourite bushranger made his last stand against the police. Kelly has been the subject of great interest, with movies, TV shows, paintings, novels and dissertations about him. A leading figure in Australian folklore, Ned was born on a small farm in Victoria, in 1854 to an Irish convict father, the oldest of 8 children. The police constantly harassed his father who died in prison when Ned was 12. Ned's life was a real 'survival of the fittest.' He spent three years in prison for robbing coaches and turned to cattle theft on his release. When a policeman made a pass at Ned's sister he was shot in the wrist and Kelly became a wanted man. In 1878 Ned formed the Kelly Gang with brother Dan and two friends, killing several police in a shootout. They eluded capture for several years, robbing banks and helping struggling farmers in *Robin Hood* style. In 1880 the police cornered the gang at Glenrowan pub. The other three were killed, but Ned wore his famous, bulletproof suit of armour that weighed 41 kilos. His legs were shot out from under him. The public mobbed the Melbourne courthouse during his trial and collected 32 000 signatures for a full pardon, but he was hanged, aged 25. Supposedly his last words were, 'Such is life.'

1906 Maria Goeppert Mayer, the German-American physicist was born in Kattowitz, Germany. She held build the first atomic bomb. She was the first American woman to receive a Nobel Prize, which she co-shared for her work on nuclear shell theory.

1934 American Indian children were required to attend school, after the passage of the Taylor Grazing Act.

1954 Actress Alice Krige was born in Upington, South Africa. She appeared in *Barfly* and *Chariots of Fire*.

1976 The Seychelles Islands became independent after 162 years of British rule. It is a national holiday.

1997 Mike Tyson In one of the strangest boxing events ever, bit off a chunk of heavyweight challenger Evander Hollyfield's ear. Tyson was disqualified.

The makeshift suit of armour worn by Australian folk hero and bushranger Ned Kelly during his years as an outlaw from the British colonial authorities.

29 JUNE

1906: Mesa Verde National Park

The park in Colorado, considered the premier United States archeological park and a World Cultural Heritage Site, was dedicated. Native Americans lived there for at least one thousand years, building mud houses in the protective shelter of massive sandstone alcoves. Access to arable farmland was by ladder to the cliff top. Mesa Verde features about 600 buildings, ranging from storage units, to villages. It is not known why the Indians abandoned it in the late 13th century to move south.

1914: Ellen Kuzwayo

The former teacher, social worker and Member of South Africa's Parliament was born. Kuzwayo received the Soweto Milestones Award in December 2004 for her contributions to her township of Soweto, one of the centres of South African civil rights activism. Following the unrest of the late 1970s, she was appointed the sole female member of the Committee of Ten, whose job was to formulate recommendations on the running of Soweto's civic affairs, after the demise of the hated Urban Bantu Council. She was a founding member of the Urban Foundation, an innovative business activist group that pressured the apartheid government to allow land ownership and private money to flow into Soweto. The government detained her for several months without charge. On her release, the tireless Kuzwayo became a consultant to an umbrella group that oversaw all of Sweto's women's self-help groups. She served as a Member of Parliament from 1994 until 1999, when she retired, age 85.

1986: Virgin Challenges Atlantic

Sir Richard Branson set a world record for a powerboat crossing of the Atlantic. The millionaire adventurer and entrepreneur acheived the feat in his 23 m yacht the *Virgin Atlantic Challenger,* named for his airline and record company on his second attempt. Branson was denied the Blue Riband Award, held by the *SS United States* since 1952, because he broke two competition rules. He stopped to refuel and his vessel did not have a commercial maritime purpose. In 1990 the record was officially broken when the 74 m catamaran *Hoverspeed Great Britain* completed the crossing with an average speed of 36.65 knots.

1613 The Globe Theatre, built in 1598 and where many Shakespearean plays were staged, burned down in Bankside, London, possibly from a cannon shot fired during a play. A replica was built in 1997.

1909 North America's first transcontinental auto race ended in Seattle. Six cars participated, with a Ford winning the $ 2000 prize. It took two weeks.

1929 Bolivia and Peru settled a 46-year border dispute, with American President Herbert Hoover's help.

1932 A relatively peaceful coup toppled Siam's monarchy. There had been growing restlessness under the absolute monarchy that had been in power for sixty years.

1995 The Mir Russian space station and the *US Atlantis* docked in space for the first time. This was a step toward building the International Space Station.

Russia's Mir Space Station, docked to the Space Shuttle Atlantis, was photographed by the Mir-19 crew. Cosmonauts Anatoliy Y. Solovyev and Nikolai M. Budarin, Mir's commander and flight engineer, temporarily unparked the Soyuz spacecraft from the cluster of Mir elements to perform a brief fly-around.

30 JUNE

1859: Charles Blondin

The French aerialist and acrobat crossed Niagara Falls on a tightrope. More than 25 000 watched the five-minute walk. He then crossed blindfolded, followed by a crossing with a wheelbarrow. The crowd could barely believe their eyes as each stunt became more daring than the last. The 35-year-old's last two stunts were to cross with a man on his back and then to cross on stilts. On 29 August 1874 he walked across a tightrope in Sydney, Australia, while cooking and eating an omelette.

1917: Lena Horne

The American entertainer and activist was born. She began her career at 16, in Harlem's Cotton Club, as a chorus girl. She was offered bit parts in American shows as a singer or dancer, but was generally blacklisted as a 'Communist' for her activist attempts to integrate the entertainment industry, her friendship with Paul Robeson and her 'anti-American' statements. When she married a white man they moved to Paris, as France was more tolerant of interracial marriages than America. In 1981, she performed on Broadway in *Lena Horne: The Lady and Her Music*. Contemporary artists acknowledge her contributions in breaking down racial barriers that finally allowed African-American performers to use the front door, stay in any hotel and use the hotel dining room.

1997: China reclaims Hong Kong

The British flag at Government House, Hong Kong, was lowered at 4.00 pm, followed by speeches from the Prince of Wales and Chris Patten, the last British Governor. A fireworks display on the harbour preceded the formal hand over to the Chinese at midnight, ending 150 years of British occupation. When Chinese President Jiang Zemin arrived to usher in a new era at the new Convention Centre, China's flag and a new Hong Kong Administrative Region flag were raised.

1899 Cyclist Charles Murphy became the first person to pedal at a speed of a mile a minute. That became his name, Charles 'Mile a Minute' Murphy.

1908 A huge explosion over central Siberia caused black rain and seismic shocks. Hundreds of miles were illuminated. It is believed to have been a meteorite disintegrating.

1974 Mrs Martin Luther King Sr was murdered by a man who said that God told him to do it.

1983 The Twins Foundation of Providence, Rhode Island, USA was established by a group of twins. It is an international resource and research centre into twins.

1984 John N. Turner was sworn in as Canada's 17th Prime Minister. He replaced Pierre Trudeau as leader of the Liberals.

French acrobat and tightrope-walker Charles Blondin (1824–1897), real name Jean Francois Gravelet, crossing Niagara on a tightrope in 1859.

Sultry American blues and jazz singer and actress, Lena Horne, in 1947.

Above: Singer Madonna and 24-year-old student Birhan Woldu, former Ethiopian famine victim and the inspiration for Live Aid 1985, are seen on stage during 'Live 8 London' in Hyde Park on July 2, 2005 , England. Woldu's face was featured in a video at Live Aid as a dying child with only ten minutes to live before she was saved by aid workers who gave her a rehydration solution. Concerts around the world attracted nearly a million people while over three billion watched on television. The Live 8 concerts, just before the start of a G8 meeting of the world's most powerful nations, sent the message 'make poverty history', explaining that poverty in the third world is something the world's rich can rectify.

Left: A protester is handcuffed by police officers in Edinburgh, Scotland on 4 July 2005, as they break up one of several organised protests related to the G8 Summit in Gleneagles Luxury Hotel in Perthshire, Scotland.

1 JULY

2004: Royal Ex Oz

UNESCO inscribed the Royal Exhibition Building (REB) and Carlton Gardens in Melbourne, Victoria on its prestigious World Heritage Site listing. This was the first Australian building to be recognised. The country was only 91-years-old when the foundation stone was laid, which makes it even more noteworthy. The building combines elements of Italian Renaissance, Byzantine, Lombardic and Romanesque architecture, with a soaring cathedral-like dome and gilded cupola. It was built for the 1880 Melbourne International Exhibition in an era when exhibitions were a way to show off a city's prosperity and might, like Prince Albert's famous Crystal Palace of 1851. Melbourne was one of the world's most affluent cities because of recent gold discoveries.

1867: British North America Act

A new nation, Canada, was born when the British Parliament passed the *British North America Act* (BNA Act 1867). John A Macdonald was the first Prime Minister. His family had emigrated from Scotland to Ontario when he was a child. He was an attorney, before becoming politically active. He led the Conservative Party for 24 years and was able to skillfully form alliances with political opponents over religious and ethnic issues. He had great finesse in balancing the diverse interests of the huge country: French and English, rural and town dwellers and Roman Catholics and Protestants. Pressures from the American Civil War and the Conservative Party's electoral defeat made MacDonald re-think his blueprint for a federated Canada. After the 1867 elections confirmed his Prime Ministership he wrote the constitution to provide for bilingualism and federal powers to oversee currency, taxation, banking and defence, with an important clause to diminish provincial power. Despite the death of his first wife and son, the later birth of a daughter with severe defects and his own chronic alcoholism, he persevered with his plans. Defeated in 1874, he was re-elected as Prime Minister in 1878. The Canadian Pacific Railroad, which unified the country from coast to coast, was built during his tenure. Canada's 'founding father' died in office in 1891, aged 76.

1804 George Sand, pseudonym for Amandine Dupin Dudevant, was born in Paris. She wrote more than 80 books. Her reputation as a liberated woman eclipsed her writings.

1867 The Canadian Dominion was formed by Upper and Lower Canada and some of the Maritime Provinces. It is celebrated as Canada Day, a national holiday.

1952 Dan Akroyd was born in Ottawa, Ontario. He starred in Ghostbusters and Caddyshack.

1979 The first Walkman was introduced by Sony, the Japanese electronic giant. Over 200 million have been sold.

1980 Australian women permitted to join the all-male bastion Surf Lifesaving Clubs.

Singer Domingo Samudio, singer and actor Isaac Hayes and actor Dan Akroyd at the Hard Rock Cafe to celebrate the 50th Anniversary of Rock and Roll in New York City, 21 January, 2004.

2 JULY

1862: William Henry Bragg

Australia's first Nobel Prize winner was born at Westward, Cumberland, England. The prize was awarded to him and to his son, William Lawrence Bragg. William Henry Bragg studied mathematics and physics at Cambridge University. He moved to Australia to take up a position at the University of Adelaide, South Australia. He was also an instrument inventor. His son was born on 31 March, 1890 and educated in Adelaide. Using one of Bragg Senior's inventions, they collaborated in the field of X-Ray crystallography, for which they were awarded the 1915 Nobel Prize for Physics, when Bragg junior was 25-years-old.

1937: Amelia Earhart

The aviator and her navigator, Fred Noonan, disappeared in their attempt to fly around the world. They had left Oakland, California 1 June, 1937 heading east. They made a stop at New Guinea on 29 June. The next stop would have been Howland Island, then Honolulu and home. They apparently ran low on fuel, but that leaves many unanswered questions, because the sea was calm and the plane floated and they carried provisions. An intensive search revealed nothing. Earhart, born in 1897, received her pilot licence in 1922. She set 13 records including her May 1932 solo flight across the Atlantic Ocean. In 1935 she set three records, including the first solo flight between Honolulu and Oakland, California.

1982: Larry Deck Chair

Truck driver Larry Walters rigged his own flying machine—an aluminium lawn chair and 45 helium-filled weather balloons. His friends helped launch *Inspiration I* at San Pedro, California. In about 45 minutes Walters had reached 4,875 m and floated around for two hours, enjoying himself but startling airline pilots on their descent toward Los Angeles Airport. When Walters started feeling cold, he shot out some of the balloons with a pistol and gradually descended, landing a power line in Long Beach and causing a regional power blackout. His caper did not amuse the police and aviation authorities and he was fined US $1500.

1993: Weary Dunlop

Sir Edward 'Weary' Dunlop died, aged 85 in Melbourne. He was nicknamed 'Weary' as a school boy because his last name is the same as a well-known tyre company and a tyre shows 'wear' with age and mileage. Fellow prisoners-of-war looked up to him as a god when he was a POW surgeon in the Second World War on the Burma-Thailand Railroad. He risked his life many times for his patients.

1489 Thomas Crammer, English clergyman and Archbishop of Canterbury, was born at Aslacton, Nottinghampshire. A reformer, he helped write *The English Book of Common Prayer*. He was charged with treason and burned alive in 1556.

1777 Vermont, America, was the first colony to abolish slavery.

1947 An unidentified flying object crashed near Roswell, New Mexico. The US Air Force claimed it was a weather balloon; many believe it carried extra-terrestrial beings.

2000 Vicente Fox Quesada was elected Mexico's President on his 58th birthday. It was the first time in seventy years that a candidate was not elected from the Partido Revolucionario Institucional party (PRI). He is from the Partido Accion Nacional (PAN).

2002 Skandia Atlantic Spirit, the highest tech rowing boat ever built, rowed by four British men, aborted its effort to break the Atlantic Ocean crossing in under 35 days when it was damaged on day 21.

Left: Aviator Amelia Earhart in 1932.

Right: Linda Finch touches down with her Lockheed Electra 10E after an around-the-world flight that closely replicated Amelia Earhart's historic around-the-world expedition.

13 NOVEMBER

1850: Robert Louis Stevenson

The poet, novelist and essayist was born in Edinburgh. Stevenson suffered from tuberculosis as a child. He spent months in bed reading and daydreaming. He began writing at an early age and from age 21 he published essays in magazines. In 1880 he married Frances 'Fanny' Osbourne and they began a life of adventure abroad. His first popular book was *Treasure Island*. Stevenson's *The Strange Case of Dr Jekyll and Mr Hyde* sold 40 000 copies in just six months in Britain. He said that its plot came to him in a dream. In search of finding the best climate for his health, he sailed with his family to Western Samoa, where he made his home. Stevenson often travelled to Hawaii and became close friends with the Hawaiian monarchy. Stevenson published a book of poems, which soon became the classic favourite *A Child's Garden of Verses*. His novels and travel writings depicted adventure, romance and psychological intrigue and became immensely popular. At the time of his death, at age 44, Stevenson was working on *The Weir of Hermiston*, which was never completed, but thought to be one of his best works. Stevenson lived a short, prolific and full life. His stories live on in the hearts and minds of people everywhere. He is buried in Samoa where Samoans call him 'Tusitala', the teller of tales.

1942: The Sullivans

Five brothers from the Sullivan family died while serving together on the *USS Juneau* when their ship was torpedoed in the World War II. George, Francis, Joseph, Madison and Albert came from Waterloo, Iowa. The young men had insisted on serving together. The Sullivan brothers' story is often called the biggest sacrifice by one family in the history of the American Navy. Two ships were named after them. The 1944 movie *The Sullivans* tells their story and their sacrifice was the inspiration for the Steven Spielberg movie *Saving Private Ryan*. The Waterloo convention centre is named in their honour, along with a park and a memorial at their former school.

1903 France's Camille Pisarro, the 'Dean of the Impressionist painters', died. He was 73.

1907 Inventor Paul Cornu tested the world's first manned helicopter in Paris. It was uncontrollable and only flew for a few seconds.

1942 The British Army under General Bernard Montgomery captured Tobruk, Libya in World War II.

1954 Ellis Island, the American immigration station in New York's Harbor, closed. It had processed 20 million immigrants since 1892.

1977 Somalia in Southern Africa, ordered all Communist advisers out of the country. It also severed its ties with Cuba.

A circa 1880 picture of Scottish novelist, poet and traveller Robert Louis Balfour Stevenson (1850–1894). He was born in Edinburgh and after considering professions in law and engineering, he pursued his interest in writing. A prolific literary career ensued, which flourished until his death in Samoa in 1894.

14 NOVEMBER

1851: Moby Dick

Herman Melville's novel was published in America. It had been published three weeks earlier in Britain as *The Whale*, to avoid people taking offence at the title's second word. However, the publisher inadvertently omitted the essential Epilogue, which left readers and critics totally confused. *Moby Dick* is an epic tale of good and evil, of Captain Ahab's obsessive search to kill the great white whale, which tore off his leg. 'Call me Ishmael', the narrator's opening line, is one of literature's best known opening sentences. The novel was supposedly named after a real albino whale named Mocha Dick, caught in 1839. Melville's genius was not acknowledged during his lifetime and he died in poverty in 1891. Today, *Moby Dick* is considered one of the great English novels.

1889: Nellie Bly

Elizabeth Cochrane Seaman, using the Bly pseudonym, left New York to mimic Jules Verne's book, *Around the World in Eighty Days*. After seventy-two days, six hours, eleven minutes and fourteen seconds, she returned to New York, beating Verne's fictional Phileas Fogg. After refusing to write fashion and gardening stories for the *Pittsburgh Dispatch*, she moved to New York City and was hired by the *New York World*. Bly was a pioneering investigative reporter. For her first story, she committed herself to an asylum for ten days and wrote about the horrific patient treatment she witnessed. Her writing led to immediate, major reforms. Bly revolutionised journalism for women.

1948: The Prince of Wales

Prince Charles was born at Buckingham Palace, the first child of Princess Elizabeth and Prince Philip. In 1958, he became the Prince of Wales and heir-apparent. Charles attended Trinity College and the University College of Wales, followed by service in the Royal Navy. In one of the largest royal weddings ever, Charles married Lady Diana Spencer in 1981. The couple had two sons, William and Harry. They divorced in 1996. Following Princess Diana's tragic death, Charles was praised for insisting that Diana be given a royal funeral. Charles has mixed popularity. He is a patron to a long list of charities and has supported organic farming and conservation since 1984. In 2005, he married his long-time mistress Camilla Parker-Bowles.

1900 Aaron Copland, American composer, was born at Brooklyn, NY. He incorporated folk rhythms into his works, including 'Appalachian Spring 'and Fanfare for the Common Man'. He died in 1990.

1922 The British Broadcasting Company Ltd (BBC) was launched.

1947 Robert 'Nat' Young, world champion surfer was born near Sydney. He revolutionised the sport with his aggressive style. He was Australian men's champion three times between 1966–69.

1963 Greece announced it would free hundreds who had been gaoled in the Communist uprising of 1944-50.

1985 A Colombian volcano that had been dormant for 400 years erupted. It killed about 20 000 people, mainly from mudslides from ruptured dams.

Princess Elizabeth holding Prince Charles after his christening ceremony at Buckingham Palace, London.

15 NOVEMBER

1887: Georgia O'Keeffe

The popular American was born in Wisconsin. She decided to become an artist when she was a child. During her long career she went through different phases, moving from charcoal, to huge, vivid flowers in microscopic, erotic detail, such as *Black Iris*. In the 1930s and 1940s she focused on New Mexico's barren desert landscapes and sky scapes, skulls in work, such as *Cow's Skull with Red*, or *Patio with Cloud*. She died aged 99 in 1986.

1942: Daniel Barenboim

The pianist and conductor was born in Buenos Aires, Argentina. His parents were immigrant Russian Jews. They were his first teachers and Barenboim gave his first concert aged seven. When he was nine the family moved to Israel. He later studied conducting in Germany and harmony and composition with the famed Nadia Boulanger in Paris. He has had a distinguished career and has not shied away from controversy. He is opposed to Israel's occupation of the West Bank and Gaza Strip and conducts concerts in Palestine. He co-founded a West-Eastern orchestra, to bring talented classical young musicians together. Barenboim defied public censure when he performed Richard Wagner's work as an encore at a 2001 concert. He warned the audience that he intended conducting it and invited those who were uncomfortable to leave. Most of the audience supported him. Wagner has long been taboo in Israel because he was an anti-Semite and Adolf Hitler's favourite composer.

1978: Margaret Mead

The famous anthropologist died of cancer aged 77. Her book, *Coming of Age in Samoa* revolutionised anthropology when it was published in 1928. She brought more subjectivity to social anthropology than male anthropologists were accustomed to. Mead made the word 'anthropology' a household word. Mead was tiny, feisty and controversial. Married three times, her research focused increasingly on infants and child rearing. When she delivered her only child in 1939, she insisted that her doctor view a film she had made called 'First Days in the Life of a New Guinea Baby'. She made 15 field trips, wrote over 35 books and more than 1300 professional publications.

1492 Christopher Columbus noted Indians using tobacco in his journal. This was the first recorded use of tobacco.

1923 German currency collapsed after WWI. It was now at four trillion marks to one dollar. Before the war, the exchange rate was four marks to the dollar.

1952 *The Argus* a Melbourne, Australia, newspaper, was the world's first to publish colour photographs.

1940 The City of Coventry woke up to find its streets decimated by German bombs and its 14th century cathedral in ruins.

1967 Elmer McCollum, American biochemist, devised the system for labelling vitamins. He also discovered Vitamins A and B. McCollum differentiated between fat and water-soluble vitamins.

A man stands in the ruins of Coventry Cathedral after a German nighttime air-raid destroyed the centre of the city.

16 NOVEMBER

1938: George 'Willie' Hall

Setting a soccer record that still stands today, Hall scored three goals in four minutes. Hall set his record at the British Home Championship match, when Manchester United played Northern Ireland at Manchester's home field. Hall racked up another two goals in the game's second half, scoring five of the seven goals in the seven to zero victory. Only two other players have equalled Hall's five goal score for a single game: Steve Bloomer in 1896 and more recently, Malcolm MacDonald in 1975. Hall, born in 1912, was selected ten times for the English National Team between 1933-39. Hall died in 1967.

1952: Shigeru Miyamoto

Considered one of the fathers of modern video games, Miyamoto was born near Kyoto, Japan. He has created about two-dozen Nintendo games, including Mario, Donkey Kong and the Legend of Zelda. After graduating from college in industrial arts, Miyamoto began his career at Nintendo in 1980 in its art department, designing coin-operated arcade games. His Donkey Kong was an immediate worldwide success. A Donkey Kong character, Mario, has now appeared in over 100 games. He is now general manager of Ninentendo's Entertainment and Analysis Department. He writes a script first and then adds appropriate characters. In 1998, Miyamoto was the first inductee into the Academy of Interactive Arts and Sciences' Hall of Fame. Miyamoto is reputed to have said, 'Video games are bad for you? That's what they said about rock and roll.'

1972: World Heritage

UNESCO established its World Heritage Sites program. The World Heritage designation is an attempt to protect sites of out-standing importance in the common heritage of all people. The sites may be cultural or natural. They may be a building, a city, a mountain range, a lake, a desert or a wildlife region. Endangered sites can sometimes obtain funding from the World Heritage Program, especially if the site it is in a Third World country. As of late 2004, a total of 788 sites had been listed.

1384 Hedwig was crowned King of Poland, although she was a woman.

1532 The Inca Empire fell to Spain when Chief Atahualpa was taken prisoner. He was held for ransom, but was murdered.

1873 'The Father of the Blues' composer and bandleader WC Handy was born at Florence, Alabama. He said 'the blues comes from the man furthest down'. He died in 1958. He wrote 'St. Louis Blues' and 'Memphis Blues'.'

1895 Paul Hindemith, the German composer, was born at Hanau. He lived and taught in America during WWII. He died in Frankfurt in 1963.

1919 Henry Neilson Wrigley and AW Murphy made the first south-north airplane crossing from Melbourne to Darwin, Australia.

Japanese video game giant Nintendo's famous game creator Shigeru Miyamoto displays the new portable video game which features double LCD display and touch sensor 'DS' at a press preview in Tokyo in October 2004.

17 NOVEMBER

1869: The Suez Canal

The link from the Mediterranean to the Red Sea and beyond was ceremoniously opened. France's Ferdinand de Lesseps, who received permission from the Egyptian ruler, Said Pasha, had conceived it. A group of international experts worked for nearly six years to design, plan and arrange financing for the project. Construction began 25 April 1899. It took 1.5 million workers ten years to construct the 163km canal. About 14 per cent of the world's annual shipping passes through the canal, shortening the passage to India from the UK by 6000km. As a strategically important waterway, an 1888 international convention agreed that the canal would be open to all nations during war and peace. There have been at least six occasions when the convention has been violated. Italy bombed it in WWII. In 1956 Britain France and Israel attacked Egypt to prevent General Nasser from nationalising the canal, but were forced to withdraw by America. After the 1967 Arab-Israeli War, Egypt barred Israel from the canal and sunken ships blocked the canal to all users. It reopened to all but Israel in 1975. In 1979, Israeli ships were again permitted access.

1960: RuPaul

One of the world's best-known actor-singer drag queens was born in San Diego, California. RuPaul Andre Charles launched his successful career by chance, after he found a home-taped television show for 'social misfits', *The American Music Show*. He contacted the producers who invited him to appear. In the 1990s he performed on the New York City club circuit, distinguishing himself with his 'Glamazon Look'. He recorded a duet, 'Don't Go Breaking my Heart', with Elton John in 1994, which was a smash hit in Europe. In 1999 RuPaul received the Vito Russo Entertainer of the Year award from the Gay and Lesbian Alliance Against Defamation for challenging gay stereotyping. He has appeared in several movies, including the drag queen movie *To Wong Foo, Thanks for Everything Julie Newman* and several television specials.

1890 Robert JH Kiphuth, legendary swimming coach was born. His Yale team won 175 consecutive meets between 1924–37, a total of 528 races.

1913 Kaiser Wilhelm II banned the tango dance at formal German military occasions.

1913 *Louise* became the first vessel to use the Panama Canal.

1917 Auguste Rodin, sculptor died. He is best known for *The Kiss* and The Thinker. He was never satisfied with his work, constantly reworking it.

1942 Martin Scorsese, movie director,was born in Flushing, New York. His movies include *Raging Bull* and *Mean Streets*.

American transvestite entertainer RuPaul in April 2000, at Madison Square Garden in New York.

18 NOVEMBER

1836: Sullivan's Gilbert

Sir William S Gilbert was born in London. He trained as a barrister, but achieved fame as the librettist for musician Sir Arthur Sullivan. Gilbert and Sullivan's witty, melodic, nonsensical, lively operettas include *The Pirates of Penzance*, *The Mikado* and *The Gondoliers*. *HMS Pinafore*, their most popular, ran for two years. Gilbert was very explicit about how his characters should be portrayed and their relationship was often tempestuous. Sullivan was born into a musical family in 1842. In addition to the operettas, he wrote classical music and the hymn 'Onward Christian Soldiers'. Sullivan died in 1900, aged 58. Gilbert died in 1911, trying to rescue a drowning woman he was teaching to swim.

1939: Margaret Atwood

The Canadian writer was born in Ottawa, Canada. She is one of the world's foremost contemporary authors, writing more than 25 volumes of verse, fiction, short stories and non-fiction. Her first published poetry collection, *The Circle Game*, won the Governor-General's Award. Other works include her futuristic *The Handmaid's Tale* and *Cat's Eye*. *Blind Assassin* won the Man Booker Prize. She uncannily forecasts public preoccupations, which makes her work of worldwide interest.

2004: Dame Barbara Cartland

The most prolific writer of the 20th century, Cartland wrote 720 novels, cook books and biographies. Her publisher announced on this day that Cartland had left 160 unpublished romance novels. One book is to be released monthly for the next thirteen years on the internet. Cartland's favourite colour was pink; even her dogs were dyed pink. The unpublished manuscripts were tied with pink ribbon and called *The Barbara Cartland Pink Collection*. Cartland's stories are a formulaic retelling of Cinderella, of a girl selected by a rich, handsome, titled man to be his bride. Her books always ended at the bedroom door. She sold about a billion books in 40 languages. At age 77, she began producing one every two weeks because the demand for her books was so huge. She wrote until just before her death at age 98 in 2000.

1840 The Eden, the last convict transport to Sydney, unloaded 267 men.

1878 Seamen in NSW, Victoria and Queensland went on strike against the number of Chinese working on coastal vessels. This was part of the escalating anti-Orientalism in Australia.

1928 New Zealand's Harold Williams, foreign editor for the *London Times*, spoke 58 languages, plus dialects. He was one of the greatest linguists ever.

1976 Man Ray, the American Dadaist painter and photographer, died, aged 86.

1991 Terry Waite is returned to Britain after being held prisoner by Lebanese terrorists for 1,760 days.

British Archbishop of Canterbury's Special Envoy Terry Waite relaxes on the Beirut seafront surrounded by heavily armed bodyguards from the Druze Socialist Progressit Party (PSP). Waite negotiated the release of several western hostages in Lebanon in the 1980s before being captured in January 1987 and imprisoned for nearly five years.

19 NOVEMBER

1863: Gettysburg Address

American President Abraham Lincoln delivered his eloquent speech at the dedication of the Gettysburg National Cemetery, Pennsylvania, where one of the Civil War's bloodiest battles was fought. Noted orator Edward Everett preceded Lincoln and spoke for two hours. Lincoln, in contrast, spoke for less than two minutes and said, 'In a larger sense we cannot dedicate, we cannot consecrate, we cannot hallow this ground. The brave men, living and dead, who struggled here, have consecrated it far above our power to add or detract. The world will little note, or long remember, what we say here, but it can never forget what they did here. It is for us, the living, rather to be dedicated here to the unfinished work, which they who fought here have thus far so nobly advanced. It is rather for us to be here dedicated to the great task remaining before us … that we here highly resolve that the dead shall not have died in vain, that this nation, under God, shall have a new birth of freedom; and that government of the people, by the people and for the people, shall not perish from the earth.'

1942: Calvin Klein

The designer was born in the Bronx, New York City. He always loved sketching and designing women's clothing and attended New York's prestigious Fashion Institute of Technology. After graduation, and inspired by the urban fashions of his youth, he launched his own small clothing line in 1968 when a buyer from a major department store placed an order. Klein's line expanded to sportswear, jeans and underwear. In 1978 his 11-year-old daughter was kidnapped and held for $100 000 ransom. She was released unharmed.

1997: Seven Up

The world's first surviving septuplets were born, nine weeks premature, to Bobbi and Kenny McCaughey. The four boys and three girls were named Alexis, Brandon, Joel, Kelsey, Kenny, Natalie and Nathan. Both Alexis and Nathan have serious cerebral palsy. The multiple births were the result of fertility treatments. The Des Moines, Iowa, church congregation to which they belong assisted with round the clock scheduling of volunteers to help with the babies when they returned home from hospital. They have an older sister, Mikayla, born in 1996.

1941 The *HMAS Sydney* cruiser and the German cruiser *Kormoran* sank each other off the Western Australian coast. Seventy-seven Germans drowned and 645 Australians.

1959 The Ford Motor Company dropped its famous, ugly Edsel; fewer than 100 000 sold. It was supposed to compete with medium-priced Oldsmobiles and DeSoto.

1996 The final section of Canada's Confederation Bridge was set in place at the Northumberland Strait. It took four years to build, linking Prince Edward Island and New Brunswick. It is 12.9km long.

2001 Mana Maori Media announced that two Maori women had won world titles. Alyson Clarke won the underhand wood-chopping title and Krisy Sloane won the junior water skiing title.

Chrome monster: a 1957 Ford Edsel.

20 NOVEMBER

1948: Takahe Rediscovered

The New Zealand takahe had long been assumed extinct, as it was only seen four times between 1800 and 1900. However, on this day, scientist Geoffrey Orbell found a colony of about 250 takahe, in the South Island's Murchison Mountains. It is a flightless bird of the rail family. Once widespread throughout New Zealand, takahe were easily hunted. Since 1948, their numbers have increased and they are gradually being re-introduced to other areas. In 1953, Takahe Valley in Fiordland National Park was established for them.

1923: Nadine Gordimer

The doyenne of South African letters won the Nobel Prize for Literature in 1991. She was born near Johannesburg, to a Lithuanian father and English mother. She has published thirteen novels and thirteen collections of short stories. Her first story was published as a teenager. She meticulously scrutinises her environment in her novels, examining race relations, especially the inhumanity of apartheid, and love relationships. At times, Gordimer's work was banned in South Africa. Her best known works are *The Conservationist*, which won the Man Booker Prize, *Burger's Daughter*, which describes the struggles of the daughter of the late South African Communist Party leader, and *July's People*, which describes a world turned upside down when a white family seeks haven in a hut with July, their black servant.

1995: Sergei Grinkov

The two-time Russian Olympic gold medallist pairs skater was practising with his wife Ekaterina 'Katia' Gordeyeva when he died in her arms. They were practising in Lake Placid, New York, for the 'Stars on Ice' touring skating show. He was just 28. They had been paired since he was 15 and she was 11. Grinkov and Gordeyeva were four-time World Champions. Grinkov had complained of back pain, but showed no symptoms of coronary problems. Their size difference—he was 1.8m tall and Gordeyeva was only 40 kg—enabled them to perform complex athletic lifts and throws with exquisite grace. They were the most crowd-pleasing duo of the decade. They had one daughter, Daria. Gordeyeva wrote about her loss in *My Sergei: A Love Story*. After six years as a solo artist with Stars on Ice, she married Olympic skater Ilia Kulik and they have a daughter, Elizaveta.

1909 The Chicago Tribune tallied (American) football deaths to date for the year: 26 deaths and 70 injuries. This was before helmets and shoulder gear were used.

1953 Universal Children's Day was celebrated by more than 120 countries, designated by the United Nations General Assembly.

1985 New Zealand's Archbishop Paul Reeves became his country's first Governor-General of part-Maori origin.

1999 A disastrous fire broke out at Windsor Castle, Berkshire. Priceless art works were destroyed. It took 250 firefighters 15 hours to extinguish the flames. Over 100 rooms were damaged. A lamp shining on a curtain is believed to have been the cause.

2004 Janine Haines died in Adelaide, aged 59. As leader of the Australian Democrats, she was the first woman to head a major Australian political party.

Soviet pair Sergei Grinkov and Ekaterina Gordeyeva perform a free program during the pairs figure skating competition in the 1988 Calgary Winter Olympic Games. Grinkov and Gordeyeva won the gold medal.

21 NOVEMBER

1694: Voltaire

Francois-Marie Arouet was born in Paris. He was an influential essayist, philosopher, moralist and playwright, and wrote under the pen name Voltaire. Both hard-hitting and satirical, Voltaire went in and out of favour for his political views. He was imprisoned for a year for his criticism of the French monarchy and church. After a second imprisonment in the Bastille, he was exiled to England. Immediately upon his return, he published *Lettres philosphiques* in which he compared English and French freedoms, praising England's more tolerant government. His books were banned and Voltaire was once again exiled, this time to Cirey, where he spent 15 years. While there, he wrote several tragedies, which reinstated him at the Versailles Court and made him wealthy. When he had a falling out with King Louis XV, he accepted an invitation from Frederick the Great to live in Prussia. There he completed his *Essai sur les moeurs* and his *Dictionnaire philosophe*. Once again, Voltaire provoked controversy and for two years was stateless. He was welcomed to Switzerland but angered its intellectuals and retired to his estate. Voltaire's last two decades were his most prolific, with his outspoken attacks on tyranny and intolerance in the nobility and the church. He wrote his most popular work, the witty *Candide*, during this time. After 28 years of exile, he returned to Paris, where his play *Irene* was a huge success. He died aged 84.

1920: Bloody Sunday, Dublin

When the British occupation of Ireland came under sustained attack by the Irish Republican Army (IRA) the English enlisted ex-soldiers, dubbed the 'Black and Tans' for their distinctive uniforms. They developed a reputation for drunkenness and brutality towards the Irish populace, including the sacking of entire towns such as Limerick and Balbriggan. On 'Bloody Sunday', IRA agents killed 19 of the British Administration's assassins, called the Cairo Gang, in Dublin. Later that day, British troops fired indiscriminately into the crowd at a Dublin and Tipperary football match at Croke Park, killing 12, including a 14 year old boy and Tipperary full-back, Michael Hogan. A further 65 were wounded.

1991: Pacific Crossing, With Oars

Gerard d'Aboville rowed across the Pacific Ocean, from Choshi, Japan to Ilwaco, Washington State, America, a distance of around 10 138km. The 42-year-old Frenchman began his marathon solo row on 11 July 1991.

1695 Henry Purcell, Baroque composer, died in London, aged 36. He wrote over 100 songs and the operas *The Fairy Queen* and *Dido*.

1904 Motorised buses began replacing Paris' horse-drawn carriages.

1941 Stage and screen actress Juliet Mills was born in London. She appeared in *Nanny and the Professor* and *So Well Remembered*.

1953 The British National History Museum declared that the skull of the famous 'Piltdown Man' was a hoax.

1965 Bjork Gudmundsdottir, the singer, was born in Reykjavik, Iceland. She released her first album aged 11 and sang with anarchist punk band the Sugarcubes. In 2000 Bjork won Best Actress Award for the Cannes Film Festival's Palme d'Or movie *Dancer in the Dark*.

1995 Toy Story, the first feature-length movie created wholly by computer-generated imagery, was released.

A British soldier, policeman and two members of the Black and Tans. The Black and Tans were an armed auxiliary police force serving in Ireland during the War of Independence in the 1920s.

22 NOVEMBER

1957: Alwyn Morris

The Mohawk First Nation Olympian was born in Kahnawake, Quebec, Canada. Morris was raised by his grandparents and while watching the 1968 Mexico City Olympics told his grandfather that he would one day stand on the podium for Canada. His grandfather replied that he could, if he worked really, really hard. At high school, Morris enjoyed canoeing, but was disappointed when his coaches told him that he was too lightly built for competition. He switched to kayaking, pairing with Olympian Hugh Fisher. Fisher noticed that an eagle would appear every time they trained and had a special affinity with Morris, as though it was his ancestral guide. In 1975 they became members of the Canadian National team and competed in the pairs in the Los Angeles 1984 Olympics, where they won a bronze for the 500m. They won a gold medal in the 1000m. Morris held an eagle feather aloft for his late grandfather when he mounted the podium.

1963: JFK Shot

American President John F Kennedy was assassinated in Dallas, Texas, shocking admirers worldwide. He was killed as he rode in an open car in a motorcade. The charismatic president was only 46 years old. Just 99 minutes later, Vice President Lyndon B Johnson was sworn in as President. Shortly after the shooting, police arrested Lee Harvey Oswald and charged him with Kennedy's murder. He had fired three shots from a Texas schoolbook warehouse where he was employed. Two days later, nightclub owner Jack Ruby murdered Oswald with a single gunshot as he was being transferred to a higher security facility. Speculation continues as to whether Oswald acted alone and whether Ruby murdered him to silence him.

1997: Michael Hutchence

The Australian rock star was found dead in a Sydney hotel room. The coroner reported death by suffocation from hanging, presumably accidentally. He was preparing for his band INXS's 20th anniversary tour. They had sold more than thirty million albums since their breakthrough album *Kick*. His girlfriend, Paula Yates, mother of his daughter Heavenly Hiraani Tiger Lily, died in 2000 from an accidental heroin overdose.

1907 In the ongoing battle between steamships to break the record for the New York to London crossing, Cunard's *Mauretania* set a record for one-day travel of 624 knots. This broke sister ship, the *Lusitania's* record of 618 knots.

1943 Lebanon achieved its independence from France and celebrates it with a national holiday.

1975 Juan Carlos de Borbon succeeded Generalissimo Francisco Franco, who died two days previously. Franco had handpicked him. Western nations hoped changes would be ushered into the totalitarian regime.

1990 Margaret Thatcher stepped down as Prime Minister. She was the longest serving British Prime Minister in the 20th century, from 1979 to 1990.

2003 England won the Rugby World Cup against Australia, with 26 seconds to go. The score was 20:17.

Jacqueline Kennedy, heavily veiled, holding the hands of her two children, daughter Caroline and John Jr, following the funeral service for President Kennedy at St Matthews Cathedral.

23 NOVEMBER

1903: Enrico Caruso

The legendary tenor known as the man with the 'Golden Voice', made his American debut at the New York Metropolitan Opera House in *Rigoletto*. He would become the first singer to sell one million records. Caruso was born in Naples, Italy in 1873 and died of pleurisy there, aged 48 in 1921. He had a warm, technically perfect voice. He could sing sixty opera roles and 500 songs from memory. Caruso once said, 'Success requires a lot of breath and voice, ninety per cent memory and ten per cent intelligence, a lot of hard work and a little something in the heart.'

1934: Lew Hoad

The tennis player was born in Sydney, NSW, Australia. He was ranked in the world's top ten for five years and was number one in 1956. With his movie star looks, his extrovert personality and his aggressive play, he was extremely popular. Hoad turned professional after his second successive Wimbledon victory in 1957 and won 18 of his first 27 matches against Pancho Gonzalez, the reigning professional. Gonzalez came back to win 51:36, in spirited contests that thrilled the public. Hoad retired young with back problems and opened a tennis resort in Spain. He was inducted into the International Tennis Hall of Fame in 1980. He died aged 59 from leukemia.

1963: Dr Who?

The BBC science fiction classic first aired on UK television. It ran for 679 episodes, until 1989. The main character, Dr Who is a renegade Time Lord, an eccentric, grumpy, caring, but brilliant scientist from a distant planet. William Hartnell was the first to play the lead role. The episodes featured a mixture of fantasy, science fiction, drama and adventure. It used low budget props, which made people use their imagination. The first episodes were shot in black and white. A new series was released in 2005, 42 years later.

1923 The Australian Broadcasting Commission's first radio station, 2SB, went on the air in Sydney. It later became 2BL.

1976 Andre Malraux died in Paris. He was a writer, politician, war hero and WWII underground fighter. He held the post-war position of Minister of Culture under President Charles de Gaulle and had an enormous influence on French culture.

1979 Merle Oberon, Australian-born movie actress, died. She had a 40-year career, appearing in *Wuthering Heights* and *The Life of King Henry VIII*.

1998 The European Union lifted its worldwide export ban on British beef. It had been imposed because of fears about 'mad cow disease'.

1999 Kuwait rejected a decree permitting women the right to vote or to run for political office.

English actor Jon Pertwee (1916-1996) poses with a dalek, his nemesis in the long-running TV series *Dr Who*.

24 NOVEMBER

1859: Charles Darwin

The British natural scientist published his most famous book, *On the Origin of Species by Means of Natural Selection*. It was an immediate and controversial bestseller and was reprinted six times in a decade. Interestingly, although people refer to 'Darwin's theory of evolution' he never used the word 'evolution'. He had spent twenty years developing his theory, after he sailed on board the *HMS Beagle*, in 1831–36. His time spent in the remote Galapagos Islands was particularly important. He observed how bird and tortoise species differed from island to island and yet bore similarity to South American species 1000km away. He suggested that those that had survived had adaptive features that were inherited. This directly contradicted the biblical teaching of Creation.

1923: Denise Levertov

The Anglo–American poet was born in Essex, England. She decided to become a writer when she was five. Her mother home-schooled her and exposed her to English and American literature. She sent some poems to poet TS Eliot for his advice when she was 12 and he encouraged her with a two-page letter. At 17, Levertov's first poem was published. She immigrated to America in 1948, becoming one of the leading avante garde voices in the 1960s and 1970s, writing on feminism, liberalism and Vietnam. One of her most notable works expressing her rage was *The Sorrow Dance* (1967). Other notable collections include *With Eyes at the Back of Our Heads* (1959) and the posthumous *This Great Unknowing: Last Poems*. Her work encompasses 20 volumes of poetry, four books of prose and translations. She died of cancer in 1997.

1971: Cooper's Leap

A mysterious middle-aged man, whose aeroplane ticket was made out to 'D B Cooper', parachuted from a plane. He had with him $200 000 that he had collected as ransom for the safe release of the aeroplane crew and passengers. He jumped over a wilderness area south of Seattle, Washington, from an altitude of 3000 m. He was wearing a thin suit, raincoat and sunglasses. The outside air temperature was below zero. Several thousand dollars of the marked banknotes turned up in the Columbia River to the north, nine years later. He was never identified or found and is presumed dead.

1966 Television programmes were transmitted directly between Australia and Great Britain for the first time, using the orbiting satellite Intelsat 2.

1973 Australian Aborigines voted to elect a National Aboriginal Consultative Committee to advise the Australian government on Aboriginal issues.

1977 Greek archaeologists announced finding King Philip II's tomb at Salonika. Philip was Alexander the Great's father.

1995 Irish voters narrowly passed a referendum, by less than 1 per cent, legalising divorce.

1997 Afghanistan's rulers agreed to destroy the opium poppy crop, source of half of the world's heroin supply. However, new crops have since been planted and harvested.

1998 At the British Parliament's opening, Queen Elizabeth II outlined the Labour Party's plan to abolish the ancient rights of 700 hereditary peers in sit in the House of Lords.

British naturalist Charles Darwin (1809-1882), who developed the theory of evolution by natural selection.

25 NOVEMBER

1952: Imran Khan

The first and only Pakistan Cricket Team Captain to win a World Cup Final was born. He is considered his country's greatest cricketer, playing from 1982–88. He was a charismatic cricketer with movie star looks, who received proposals of marriage from all over the world. When President General Zia Ul Haq asked him to rejoin the team in 1991–92 an ecstatic Pakistan won the World Cup.

1970: Yukio Mishima

The distinguished writer, who was nominated three times for the Nobel Prize for Literature, committed ritual suicide publicly in Tokyo. He studied martial arts and created the Tatenokai (Shield Society), a school for young men. He was an international celebrity at the height of his literary output of about 100 works, when he led the Tatenokai in an abortive coup d'etat to restore military power to the Emperor. A fellow swordsman completed the act with a ritualistic decapitation.

1977: Prince's medals

After being lost for 30 years, war medals belonging to Canada's most decorated First Nation hero, were returned to his family. Sergeant Thomas Prince of the Salteaux people was born at Lake Winnipeg in 1915. He fought with the American Fifth Army in Italy during World War II. His task was to make night-time reconnaissance of the Germans to estimate their numbers and what he could overhear. Because life went on as usual during the war for many Italian farmers, on one occasion when it was necessary to repair a cut radio wire Prince dressed as an Italian farmer. He went first to the German–Italian line and waved his fist at them, then cursed the Allied soldiers, before beginning hoeing. When he found the break in the wire, he pretended to tie his boots and surreptitiously spliced the cable. Prince participated in other incredible exploits that earned him awards from America and Australia. He was one of only three Canadians awarded the King George V1 Military Medal. After the war he became a Manitoba land rights activist. He later fought in the Korean War with distinction. He died aged 62.

Pakistani cricketer and politician
Imran Khan.

1763 French writer Abbe Prevost died. His classic *Manon Lescaut* was made into an opera by both Giacomo Puccini and by Jules Massenet.

1920 Noted racecar driver Gaston Chevrolet was killed at 28, in a 400km car race. He was the youngest of three racing brothers. He was born in France and moved to America as a child.

1975 Suriname in South America achieved its independence from the Netherlands.

1990 Poland held its first democratic presidential election. Union leader and Solidarity founder, Lech Walesa, won.

26 NOVEMBER

1607: John Harvard

The Boston clergyman was born in London. He immigrated with his wife to the Massachusetts Bay Colony, bringing with him a library he had purchased with his inheritance. On his deathbed at 31, he bequeathed half his estate and his 300-volume library to the Colony to establish an educational institution in Newtowne. Many of the colonists, including Harvard, had been educated at England's Cambridge University, so Newtowne was renamed Cambridge. Harvard University became one of the world's most respected universities.

1910: Cyril Cusack

Considered Ireland's finest actor, Cusack was born, in Durban, South Africa, to a policeman and a chorus girl. When Cusack was six, his mother left his father and moved to Ireland, where she set up her own theatrical company. Cusack made his debut when he was seven He later said that life on the road was a 'glorious adventure'. Cusack appeared in many movies, including *My Left Foot* and *The Day of the Jackal*. His stage career included the Abbey Theatre, the Royal Shakespeare Theatre and the Old Vic. His daughters Sinead, Socha, Niamh and Catherine and some of his extended family, Jeremy Irons and Nigel Cook, are also actors. Cusack died in 1993.

2004: Cirque du Soleil

KÁ, Cirque du Soleil's new production, opened at the MGM Grand Hotel and Casino in Las Vegas, Nevada. It cost $165 million to stage and was expected to bring in $US2 million a week. From street performer beginnings in Montreal, Guy Laliberte and Gilles Ste-Croix built Cirque du Soleil into a billionaire-dollar empire. Between 1984 and 1989 the Cirque had one touring show, with 270 000 ticket sales. By 2003, the Cirque had nine touring shows on three continents with an audience of seven million. No language and no animals are used and the costuming and music are always breathtaking.

1857 The first Australian Parliament opened in Melbourne.

1966 French President Charles de Gaulle opened the world's first tidal-power generating station at the Rance estuary in Brittany.

1997 Iraqi leader Saddam Hussein invited foreign experts to live in his 'presidential palaces', to prove he was hiding nothing, but declared the palaces were off-limits to weapons inspectors.

1998 The Supreme Court of Canada ruled that authorities had the right to search primary and secondary school students without a search warrant.

2001 Nepal's King Gyandera imposed a state of emergency after Maoist rebels, trying to unseat the monarchy, killed more than 100 people in three days. Unrest continues.

Cirque de Soleil's *Zumanity* performs on a special *Tonight Show* at the Paris Hotel and Casino in Los Angeles, California.

27 NOVEMBER

1942: 'Scuse Me While I Kiss the Sky

James Marshal Hendrix was born in Seattle, Washington, an American of African, European, Cherokee Indian and Mexican descent. Revered for his flashy yet soulful guitar style, Hendrix was discovered by Chas Chandler, bass player for The Animals. Hendrix with Noel Redding on bass and Mitch Mitchell on drums formed The Jimi Hendrix Experience and released their first single, 'Hey Joe', in December 1966. In May of 1967, the group released their first album, *Are you Experienced?* Jimi Hendrix tragically died in his sleep on September 18 1970, at the height of his popularity. His smash hit, 'Voodoo Child', was released posthumously and shot straight to the top of the charts.

2000: Longest Tunnel

Norway's King Harald opened the world's longest tunnel in Laerdal. It is 24.5km long and avoids twisting roads over a mountain range and a ferry ride. Blue lights at intervals illuminate the roof and yellow lights at the base give drivers the illusion of being outdoors. Three 30-m-wide caverns in the middle of the tunnel can act as a turning area in case of a fire blocking one end. The tunnel has highly sophisticated monitoring devices. The Gotthard, the world's second longest tunnel, through the Alps between Italy and Switzerland, is 16.3km long and took eleven years to build. It saves drivers 30km of mountain driving through snowy passes that can be impassable.

2003: Stick It, Mr Blair

Benjamin Zephaniah said 'Stick it, Mr Blair' and 'Mrs Queen, stop going on about the Empire', when asked why he had turned down an Officer of the Order of the British Empire (OBE) award from Queen Elizabeth II. Usually acceptance or rejection of honours is private, but the outspoken poet used it as a platform to denounce British colonial history. A Rastafarian, he is one of the UK's most original and well-known poets. Born the oldest of nine children in Birmingham, Zephaniah was an undiagnosed dyslexic, who did not learn to read or write until he was in his twenties. He committed petty crimes and was imprisoned. When he discovered Percy Bysshe Shelley's radical poetry, Zephaniah began writing and performing. His work is a mixture of the dissenting Romantic poets and modern punk rapping. He believes that dissenters who accept honours have been 'had' by the establishment. Zephaniah said, 'Whoever is behind this (OBE offer) can never have read any of my work.'

1889 The Great Hall of Sydney Town Hall, one of Australia's superb buildings, opened.

1907 Aviator Alberto Santos–Dumont wore the first wristwatch made especially for him by Louis Cartier. Previously, watches were worn on a chain.

1911 When J M Synge's *The Playboy of the Western World* premiered in New York, the Irish actors were pelted with vegetables. The audience did not appreciate Synge's bitter humour.

1942 The French Navy scuttled its ships at Toulon to keep them out of Nazi Germany's hands.

2000 Sri Lanka's Liberation Tigers of Tamil Eelam, after seventeen years of civil war, said they were prepared to hold unconditional peace negotiations in an attempt to end the conflict. Unrest continues.

Musician Jimi Hendrix (1942–1970) plays at the Isle of Wight Music Festival, England in June 1970. He died a few months later.

28 NOVEMBER

1895: First Car Race

Expecting only a handful of entrants for their 'horseless carriage' race, the *Chicago Times-Herald* was amazed to learn that over 70 inventors were eager to participate in America's first automobile race, held on this day with a US$2000 prize. The field was whittled down to six. J Frank Duryea won the 86km race, from Chicago to Evanston, Illinois, in about ten hours, at an average speed of 11.5km/h. The vehicles were called automobiles, cars, locomobiles and motor vehicles. Duryea and his brother Charles, who built the first petrol-powered car, expanded their business and later built luxury Stevens-Duryea limousines. The race led to a growth in vehicle design and manufacture. There were three-wheelers, four- wheelers and the famous 1897 steam-powered Stanley Steamers. By the time Henry Ford set up his factory in 1903, the Stanley factory already employed about 150.

1954: Enrico Fermi

The Italian physicist died, aged 53. Born in Rome, Fermi was curious about everything as a child. A teacher told him that he was destined to be an extraordinary scientist. He won a Nobel Prize in Physics for his work in 1938, then immediately immigrated to America with his Jewish wife to escape the rampant anti-Semitism of the Fascist Government. Fermi and his team built the first atomic chain reactor from a pile of uranium and graphite on the University of Chicago's squash court. This led to the first atomic bomb, which was tested in New Mexico in 1945 and weeks later was used on Hiroshima and Nagasaki, in Japan.

1999: Hsing-Hsing

The only panda at Washington's National Zoo was euthanased after being ill for a long time. He was 28, far older than a panda would normally live for. Hsing Hsing and his mate Ling Ling were a gift from China to America in 1972. They had no cubs. Since then, pandas Mei Xiang and Tian Tian have been loaned to the National Zoo for ten years. Both China and the San Diego Zoo have succeeded in breeding captive pandas. It is one of the world's most endangered animals.

1520 Portuguese navigator Ferdinand Magellan reached the Pacific Ocean, from the Atlantic Ocean. The Magellan Strait is named after him.

1875 The first champagne produced in Australia was introduced in Sydney.

1905 The nationalist Sinn Fein Party was founded in Dublin, Ireland.

1919 'Well done, Mum' said Lady Astor's 12-year-old son when he heard she was the first woman elected to the British Parliament. She was a Conservative, committed to women and children's rights.

1985 Social historian Fernard Braudel and founder of *Les Annales,* the first journal of social history, died aged 83. He wrote multi-volume works on 15-18th century history.

Hsing-Hsing, the National Zoo's only giant panda, in Washington in June 1999. Hsing-Hsing was put to sleep on 28 November 1999, after months of failing health due to kidney disease.

29 NOVEMBER

1832: Louisa May Alcott

The author was born in Philadelphia, Pennsylvania, on her father's birthday. Amos Bronson Alcott had enormous influence on his daughter. He was an educational reformer who believed in women receiving a sound education and having the freedom to vote. He was also a staunch anti-slavery advocate. Louisa enjoyed writing dark stories of mayhem and angst, but when the Alcotts needed money, she changed her theme and writing style. She is best remembered for her classic *Little Women*, which portrayed family life and its hardships. The characters Meg, Beth and Amy were modelled on her sisters and Jo was modelled on herself. The book sold well and she was able to pay off the family debts. She died in 1888 in Boston, two days after her father.

1898: Jack O'Hagan

The prolific composer of sheet music during the WWII era was born in Melbourne Victoria. His songs include 'Our Don Bradman' and three songs about a small country town, Gundagai, NSW, which he never visited: 'On the road to Gundagai', 'When a boy from Alabama meets a girl from Gundagai' and 'Where the dog sits on the tucker box (Five Miles from Gundagai)'. The latter is still sung today and there is a monument to the famous dog there. In the 1880s an unknown poet first wrote about the dog that sat patiently guarding a tucker box (lunch pail) while his owner tried to get a bullock team out of a muddy river crossing, nine miles (not five) from Gundagai.

2000: Blue Mountains Heritage

The Greater Blue Mountains of New South Wales were listed as a World Heritage Area. It consists of six national parks and four wilderness areas, covering 1 million hectares of sandstone cliffs, deep gorges, rivers and eucalyptus forests. The eucalyptus oil causes a blue haze, hence the name Blue Mountains. It has a biodiversity that makes it recognised as one of the planet's most unique and beautiful places. It includes 14 000-year-old Aboriginal rock carvings and rare and endangered species, including the Wollemi pine. The Blue Mountains attract more than 3 million tourists annually who come to sightsee, hike and rock-climb.

View from Evan's lookout, near Blackheath, in the majestic Blue Mountains of Australia.

1946 Brian Cadd, Australian singer and songwriter was born in Perth. He wrote for the highly successful bands Groop and Axiom. Cadd went solo and is one of Australia's most prolific songwriters. His 'Arkansas Grass' is a classic.

1985 'Crack', a new type of cocaine, was announced to be showing up in New York City.

1999 Northern Ireland's rival religion-based political parties formed a Protestant–Roman Catholic Government. It was the first time the bitter enemies had shared power.

2001 Representatives of thirty countries and of the diamond industry, met to discuss ways to ensure legitimate diamond shipments. It was an attempt to weed out illegitimate shipments whose proceeds were used to fund African civil wars.

30 NOVEMBER

1835: Mark Twain

Samuel Langhorne Clemens, pen name Mark Twain, was born. He spent his early years by the Mississippi River in Hannibal, Missouri. His father died when he was 11 and he left school to work. He was apprenticed to a printer and began writing at 13. For four years he was a steamboat pilot, earning enough to become an adventurer and gold miner. He turned to full-time writing, using the name Mark Twain, meaning 'two fathoms deep'. He wrote *Tom Sawyer, The Prince and the Pauper* and *the Adventures of Huckleberry Finn*, plus travel books and short stories, including *The Celebrated Jumping Frog of Calaveras County*. Twain was known for his wit. On seeing his obituary in a newspaper, he famously said, 'The reports of my death are greatly exaggerated'. He died on 21 April 1910.

1981: ABBA

ABBA's eighth and last album *The Visitors*, was released. The name ABBA was created from the initials of the two married Swedish couples, Agnetha and Bjorn and Ani-Frid and Benny. They are now divorced. ABBA was one of the most popular groups in the 1970s, with hits such as 'Waterloo', 'I Do, I Do, I Do, I Do, I Do' and 'Dancing Queen'. They still have a huge cult following and their music has featured in several Australian movies such as *Priscilla, Queen of the Desert* and *Muriel's Wedding*.

1987: James Baldwin

The noted African–American writer died of stomach cancer in Saint Paul-de-Vence, France, where he had lived in self-imposed exile. His writing described growing up black in America. His best known work, *Go Tell It on the Mountain*, was published in 1953 when he was 29. He also wrote *The Fire Next Time, Nobody Knows My Name* and others. He returned to America in the 1960s during the civil rights movement, where he was criticised by his fellow African–Americans for not being more militant and for addressing homosexuality in his writing. He was born in New York City, the eldest of nine children. His stepfather was a minister and gospel cadences show through in his writing. Baldwin wrote, 'Colour is not a human or personal reality. It is a political reality.'

1667 Jonathan Swift, Irish satirist and clergyman, was born in Dublin. He wrote the ever-popular *Gulliver's Travels*. He died in 1745.

1901 Edward Eyre, the English explorer, died aged 86, after spending many years in Australia. He crossed the Nullabor Plain in 1840–41 to Western Australia. He also was a colonial administrator in New Zealand and the West Indies.

1916 Austrian Emperor Franz Joseph died. His rule spanned 68 years. He tried and failed, to hold his 17-nation Empire together. He lost Italy and Germany and weakened the hold on Hungary. The Emperor's successor was Carl Francis Joseph, aged 29, the younger brother of Archduke Franz Ferdinand, whose assassination triggered WWI.

1966 The Caribbean nation of Barbados gained its independence from Great Britain.

1999 40 000 anti-globalism protesters brought Seattle, Washington to a stand still where the World Trade Organization meeting was held. The meeting was organised via email.

American humourist and writer Samuel Clemens (1835–1910) who wrote under the pen name of Mark Twain.

Opposite: An authentic steam-powered river boat on the Mississippi River, in New Orleans, Louisiana.

1 DECEMBER

1951: Sir Peter Buck

Te Rangi Hiroa (Peter Buck) died aged around 71 in Honolulu, Hawaii (his date of birth is uncertain). Buck was a true Renaissance man; he excelled in athletics, pursued a medical career, served in the military with the First Maori Contingent in World War I and held elected and civil service posts in New Zealand's Government. Buck was one of the earliest ethnologists and anthropologists to focus on Polynesia. He was the author of several classics, including *Vikings of the Sunrise*. He was appointed Professor of Anthropology at Yale University and later, director of the Bishop Museum in Honolulu. His ashes were returned to his ancestral home at Taranaki, New Zealand.

1952: Christine Jorgensen

George Jorgensen announced her male to female gender re-assignment. It was a media sensation, although she was not the first person to have sex change surgery. The 26-year-old blond, blue-eyed beauty became the spokesperson for transsexual and trans-gendered people. It took the former soldier six operations at a Copenhagen hospital and 2000 hormone injections to complete her transformation.

1955: Civil Rights

When 42-year old Rosa Parks refused to give up her seat to a white man on a public bus, she was arrested in Montgomery, Alabama. Her arrest led to boycotts and legal action to end racial discrimination in the segregated South. After Parks' arrest, Martin Luther King Jr launched the Montgomery Bus Boycotts. African-Americans boycotted the bus system, enduring personal hardship such as walking miles daily for almost a year, rather than ride the bus. Parks' individual action became a symbol of the power of civil disobedience. Nonviolent protest continued to be used by ordinary citizens to challenge segregation throughout the Civil Rights Movement. In 1956 the United States Supreme Court ruled that segregated bus services were unconstitutional. For her lifetime of civil rights activism, Parks was awarded the US Congressional Gold Medal in 1999.

1898 Movie-making began in New Zealand when the Auckland Exhibition was filmed by AH Whitehouse, an itinerant filmmaker.

1900 Nicaragua sold its rights to the Panama Canal to the United States, for US$5-million.

1910 Wassily Kandinsky, the Russian painter, said that he questioned the whole basis of modern art, believing that colours had their own life and that they all 'obey a close contact with the human soul.'

1988 Benazir Bhutto was named Pakistan's Prime Minister, the first woman to lead a modern-day Muslim country.

2001 Japan's Crown Prince Naruhito and his wife, Princess Masako, gave birth to their first child, a daughter.

This page: Former soldier and transsexual, Christine Jorgensen, at a press reception at the London Pavillion in 1970.

Top left: Rosa Parks (in dark coat and hat) rides a bus at the end of the Montgomery bus boycott, in Montgomery, Alabama, December 26, 1956.

Bottom left: The bus on which American civil rights activist Rosa Parks was arrested, sparking the bus boycott, now preserved in the Henry Ford Museum in Dearborn, Michigan.

2 DECEMBER

1953: Snowy Baker

Australia's Reginald Leslie 'Snowy' Baker, one of the most versatile sportsmen, died aged 69. Despite his wide-ranging accomplishments, he has largely been forgotten. Born in Sydney in 1884, Snowy decided that the best way to become famous was through sports. Snowy was a non-drinker and health fanatic who played on Australia's Rugby Union international team and was a talented equestrian rider. He excelled in 26 different sports including football, swimming, diving, riding, rowing and boxing. He represented Australia in the Olympics in three different events, taking the silver in boxing. Baker was also a writer, producer, silent movie star and stuntman. He worked with Charlie Chaplin in Hollywood and taught Elizabeth Taylor how to ride for *National Velvet*. He is even credited with teaching screen idol Rudolf Valentino how to kiss.

1995: Trader loses Barings

Nick Leeson, who lost £850 million as Chief Trader for Barings Bank, England's oldest bank, was imprisoned for six and a half years. Leeson's actions wiped out the 233-year-old bank, which included Queen Elizabeth II as a client. The bank was sold for £1. Leeson fled from Singapore and went into hiding before being arrested and tried. Investigations showed that Barings lacked a system of scrutiny and for double-checking trades. Leeson wrote the book *Rogue Trader* from which a movie was made. He was released early from jail after being diagnosed with colon cancer .

2004: Dame Alicia Markova

The British ballerina died aged 94, in Bath, England. She popularised ballet in the UK and America. Her title role in *Giselle* is indelibly linked with her. Born in London, 1911 as Lillian Alice Marks, she changed her name to the more Russian-sounding Alicia Markova at age 14, when she joined Diaghilev's Ballets Russes. She became a prima ballerina in 1933. She danced the leading roles in *Swan Lake, The Nutcracker* and *Giselle*. She had a major impact on ballet in the UK, founding several companies. Markova retired in 1963. She spent the rest of her life coaching young ballerinas, primarily at the Royal Ballet.

1876 Grace Bussell, the 16-year-old, heroically rescued many passengers on horseback when the *SS Georgette* ran aground at Busselton in Western Australia.

1901 Businessman King Camp Gillette patented a new razor to replace the former 'cut-throat.' It was a disposable, two-bladed 'safety' razor.

1960 Australia lifted its embargo on iron ore exports to Japan, leading to rapid expansion of the iron ore industry in Western Australia.

2001 Texas-based Enron Corp, America's largest energy-trading company, filed for bankruptcy protection. It was the largest bankruptcy in American history and had major international repercussions.

Alicia Markova (Lilian Alicia Marks) in *Swan Lake* in 1954.

3 DECEMBER

1854: The Eureka Stockade

The most celebrated rebellion in Australian history began on Bakery Hill, Ballarat. It is as symbolic for Australians as France's storming of the Bastille is for the French or the Boston Tea Party for the Americans. After the discovery of gold in Victoria the government imposed strict licence fees on miners, even if no gold was found. In protest the miners erected a stockade and flew a new flag; the Southern Cross. The Eureka rebellion was a short lived revolt against petty officialdom by poorly armed civilians. When the stockade was stormed by government forces, 30 miners and six soldiers died. More than 100 miners, 'Diggers,' were tried; thirteen were charged with high treason. All were acquitted and the fees replaced by a fairer export duty. The rebellion led to political and personal benefits for Australians and is often cited as the birthplace of Australian democracy.

1947: End of Desire

When the curtain closed on the Broadway premiere of Tennessee Williams' *A Streetcar Named Desire* the audience applauded with a thirty-minute standing ovation. At the time 23, Marlon Brando, who portrayed Stanley Kowalski, is considered to be the greatest American actor, by critics, peers and fans. *The Desire* was an actual streetcar which last ran in 1948 and was replaced by a bus line named *Desire*. Williams received a Pulitzer Prize for the play and Elian Kazan's movie version received twelve Oscar nominations. Critics would later call the play the best of the 20th century.

1984: The Bhopal Disaster

The world's worst industrial accident left more than 3000 dead and an estimated 150 000 to 600 000 injured in Bhopal, India. At least another 15 000 later died from their injuries. Safety procedures were apparently ignored at the Union Carbide (UC) pesticide plant, allowing deadly gas to escape. The Indian government sued UC in 1989 on behalf of 500 000 victims. It settled for $470 million in damages, but most survivors were never compensated. Recent allegations state that UC was importing untested technology to their Indian plant. Warren Anderson, UC's chairman at the time was declared a fugitive from justice for not appearing before the Indian courts. On the tragedy's anniversary each year, effigies of Anderson are burned. The Bhopal toxic waste has not been cleaned up and contamination remains active today. Cancer rates continue to escalate.

1895 Psychoanalyst Anna Freud was born in London. She was especially interested in children and the ego. She was Sigmund Freud's daughter and died in 1982.

1910 Neon lighting, invented by physicist Georges Claude, made its debut at the Paris Motor Show.

1917 Miriam Waddington, the poet and social worker, was born in Winnipeg, Canada. Her books include *The Visitants* and *The Glass Trumpet*.

1925 During World War 1, Australia banned immigration from certain countries. After the war, the ban was lifted on Turkey, Germany, Hungary, Austria and Bulgaria.

1975 The journal Cancer Research reported the preliminary findings that diet resulted in half of all human cancers. It identified animal fats, alcohol and contaminants as causes.

This December 1984 photo shows victims who lost their sight after poison gas leaked from a pesticides plant in the central Indian city of Bhopal, sitting in front of the American Union Carbide factory.

4 DECEMBER

1860: Charles Dickens

The first serialised instalment of *Great Expectations* was published. Dickens wrote the novel to raise money to buy a house for his wife and ten children. *Great Expectations* was one of the most popular autobiographical novels ever, with 100 000 newspaper readers eagerly awaiting each day's instalment. Dickens achieved unprecedented popularity worldwide during his lifetime for *Pickwick Papers*, *Oliver Twist*, *David Copperfield*, *A Christmas Carol* and *Our Mutual Friend*. His writing provides compelling insights into life in Victorian England. Dickens' opens *A Tale of Two Cities* with the line 'It was the best of times. It was the worst of times,' a reference to the period, which is frequently quoted. He died suddenly in 1870 at Gad's Hill, England, aged 68 and was buried in Westminster Abbey. People filed by his grave for three days to pay their respects.

1998: Space Endeavour

In a joint US-USSR effort, a space milestone was achieved when the US space shuttle *Endeavour* deployed a major section of the International Space Station. Space-walking astronauts and cosmonauts attached it to a previously deployed Russian component. It took another 45 launches and five years to build the Station. It measures 108m long by 88m wide and was designed for a seven person resident crew.

1998: Killing Fields

The last remaining Khmer Rouge fighters and commanders surrendered, ending Cambodia's brutal period of war and genocide. After intense 'carpet bombing' of Cambodia by American bombers reduced public support for the Lon Nol regime, the Khmer Rouge won their insurgency and renamed Cambodia as Democratic Kampuchea. Pol Pot's extremist regime outlawed religion, closed schools and hospitals, abolished currency, confiscated private property and relocated people to forced labour camps. The camps were known as 'Killing Fields' and formed the basis for the movie *The Killing Fields*.. Intellectuals and people wearing glasses were executed. Starvation, killing and lawlessness were rampant and over two million people were killed —a quarter of Cambodia's population. Pol Pot's government fell to a coalition of Cambodian rebels and Vietnamese soldiers and United Nations-supervised elections were held in 1993. A government was formed in 1998 and Pol Pot was found guilty of genocide. He died shortly after being condemned to life imprisonment. Many Khmer Rouge leaders have never been tried.

1154 Pope Adrian IV was the first and only English Pope.

1791 The Observer, a revered British newspaper, was published for the first time. It is the world's oldest Sunday newspaper.

1976 Lord Benjamin Britten, the English composer, died aged 62. He wrote *Peter Grimes*, *Billy Budd* and *Death in Venice*.

1996 Alan Bond, once one of Australia's wealthiest men and financier of Australia II's 1983 America's Cup winning syndicate, pleaded guilty to charges of dishonesty and $1.2 billion fraud. He was bankrupted and served four years in prison.

2002 Indonesian police arrested a Muslim cleric on charges of masterminding the Bali nightclub bombings that killed about 200 tourists and Balinese.

English novelist Charles Dickens.

5 DECEMBER

1933: Prohibition Ends

There was widespread cheering in America to celebrate the repeal of the 18th Amendment, by the 21st Amendment to the Constitution. The 18th Amendment had been ratified 16 January 1919 after years of campaigning. It had stated: 'After one year from the ratification of this Article the manufacture, sale, or transportation of intoxicating liquors within, the importation thereof into, or the exportation thereof from the United States and all territory subject to the jurisdiction thereof for beverage purposes is hereby prohibited.' The 18th was impossible to enforce. Instead of discouraging the drinking of alcoholic beverages, it actually led to new problems, with organised crime, bootleggers, speakeasies and home breweries. People smuggled alcohol into nightclubs in flasks and even inside hollow walking canes. The 'noble experiment' to control people's behaviour failed miserably. In the end it was the promise of the tax revenue that a legal liquor industry would generate during the Great Depression that convinced Franklin D Roosevelt, who never hid his fondness for martinis, to call for Prohibition's repeal.

1938: Albert Namatjira

The famed Aboriginal artist held his first solo exhibition in Melbourne. Namatjira was the first indigenous artist to paint in a Western style. Born into the Western Arrernte tribe near Alice Springs in Central Australia in 1902, he painted more than 2000 water-coloured landscapes. A painting school, the Hermannsburg Mission School, was formed to encourage Aboriginal artists and help find markets for their work. A thriving cottage industry of Aboriginal art, both in the Western style and the ancient totemic symbolic 'X-Ray' style emerged and was enthusiastically embraced by collectors. In 1957 Namatjira was ironically granted Australian citizenship, granting him the right to vote, a status denied to other Aboriginal people at the time. Namatjira was a tormented man, caught between his Aboriginal tribal values and the white community. On occasion he unwittingly ran afoul of white laws. He was awarded the Queen's Coronation Medal in 1953. He died 8 August 1959 in Alice Springs.

2001: Sir Peter Blake

Pirates murdered New Zealand's iconic 53-year-old yachtsman. He won the America's Cup twice, in 1995 and 2000, and the Whitbread round-the-world race. A record-breaking non-stop circumnavigation in 1994 earned him the Jules Verne Trophy. He was an environmental activist and adventurer, who explored Antarctica and the rivers of South America. In 1997 Sir Blake was appointed captain of the prestigious Cousteau Society, taking up the challenge to educate people about the world's ecosystems. Petty thieves murdered him on his boat *The Seamaster* at the Brazilian mouth of the Amazon River, off Macapa. He was in the region monitoring the effects of global warming and pollution for the United Nations Environment Program.

1782 Martin Van Buren, America's 8th president, was born in Kinderhook, New York. He was the first President born in America. He died in 1862.

1934 Mustafa Kemal Ataturk 'the Father of Turkey' pursued a westernisation program. Parliament granted women's suffrage and election rights.

1966 Radio Hautaki began pirate transmissions from a vessel beyond the legal limits to break the radio monopoly in New Zealand.

1994 Chechnya: Russia sealed the border of the neighbouring republic. Later troops and armoured tanks rolled in to try to restore Moscow's control of the region. Chechnya is still occupied by Russian troops, fighting a desperate coalition of independence forces.

1996 Telstra: A bill was passed in the Australian Parliament to privatise one-third of the telecommunications giant.

Model Rachel Hunter and World Sports Academy member and yachtsman Peter Blake at the Laureus Night of Sport and Film at the Monte Carlo Beach Club Hotel in 2001.

6 DECEMBER

1803: Susanna Moodie

The author was born in Bungay, Suffolk, England. As a child, Moodie was well educated but impoverished. Her father died prematurely, leaving a widow and eight children. The six daughters all began writing to help support the family. She married JWD Moodie and emigrated to Lakefield, in Ontario, Canada, to take up a military land grant in 1932. She continued writing articles, short stories, novels and poetry. She died at her daughter's home in Toronto, aged 82, in 1885. Her work was rediscovered in 1970, when Margaret Atwood published Moodie's poetry, *The Journals of Susanna Moodie*. Moodie's memoir of life on the Upper Canadian frontier, *Roughing It In the Bush*, is a literary classic.

1921: Agnes McPhail

In the first election in which women were allowed to vote and run for office, McPhail became the first woman elected to the Canadian House of Commons. Born in Windsor, Ontario in 1890, she became a school teacher interested in agriculture and became politically active when nominated as a spokesperson for the United Farmers of Ontario. She was the first woman sent as a representative to the League of Nations in Geneva. McPhail fought for human rights, prison reform and farm co-operatives. As an active member of the World Disarmament Community, she opposed war and fought for Canada's disarmament. In 1951, one of her final achievements was legislation that mandated equal pay for equal work for women. McPhail died in 1954 in Toronto aged 63. At the time of her death, she was under consideration for a seat in the Canadian Senate.

2002: Bigfoot

Scotland has its Loch Ness Monster, Australia has Yowies and America had Bigfoot—except that Bigfoot was confirmed to be a hoax on this day. Ray Wallace is now known to be the person behind Bigfoot. When Wallace died at 84 in Centralia, California his relatives revealed that Bigfoot was a practical joke. Forty-four years before, in August 1958, Wallace played pranks on co-workers in Humboldt County, California by leaving a trail of 40cm footprints made with a wooden template. The local newspaper ran the story calling the animal footprints 'Bigfoot.' Wallace later persuaded his wife to dress up in a Bigfoot suit for photographs that 'confirmed' Bigfoot's existence. A friend, Roger Patterson, shot the famous footage of the elusive, gorilla-like creature in 1967. Despite Wallace's deathbed confession, diehards still believe there is a Bigfoot out there.

1988 Roy Orbison, one of country and rock music's superstars, died in Nashville, Tennessee. His sad songs, like *Only the Lonely* and *Crying*, resonated with audiences worldwide. He was an inductee of both the Songwriters and the Rock and Roll Hall of Fame.

1992 Hindu extremists destroyed an ancient Muslim shrine in northern India prompting months of Muslim-Hindu riots that killed 2000 people.

2002 Exxon Mobil: A federal court in Alaska fined the corporation US$4 billion in punitive damages for the March 1989 *Prince William Sound* oil tanker catastrophe.

2003 Miss Ireland, Rosanna Davison, was crowned Miss World in China's first international beauty pageant.

2004 The River Murray, in drought-stricken Australia, was reported to have reached it's lowest level since records began 100 years previously.

American rock musician Roy Orbison plays acoustic guitar in a promotional portrait for director Michael Moore's film *The Fastest Guitar Alive*.

7 DECEMBER

1941: Pearl Harbour

The Japanese bombed the bulk of the American Pacific fleet, at anchor in Oahu, Hawaii, at exactly 7.55am in a surprise attack. Almost 2500 Americans lost their lives. Numerous aircraft and battleships were destroyed. The battleship *USS Arizona* exploded and sank with 1100 of its crew. The ship still lies at the bottom of Pearl Harbour as a memorial to those that lost their lives. The next day American President FD Roosevelt called the tragedy 'a date which will live on in infamy' and asked the American Congress for a declaration of war against Japan. The attack brought America into World War II, hastening victory for the Allies.

1995: Galileo

The American spacecraft successfully entered the orbit of the planet Jupiter. It was launched over six years previously, in 1989. *Galileo* released probes to study three of Jupiter's moons and sent back information showing the presence of organic compounds that could conceivably support life. It made 11 orbits around Jupiter. Its mission was then extended and it flew by Jupiter's moons: Europa, Callisto, Io, Amalthea, Thebe, Metis and Ganymede. It proved that Io was the most active body in the solar system and sent back astonishing photographs. In September 2003 *Galileo* self-destructed by plunging into Jupiter. The spacecraft was named *Galileo* after the Italian astronomer Galileo Galilei who had discovered the four great moons of Jupiter.

2004: Tana Umaga

The first Pacific Island-born captain of the All Blacks, New Zealand's Rugby team, won the International Fair Play Award, the Pierre de Coubertin Trophy. The award was for Jonathan Falefasa 'Tana' Umaga's 'sportsmanlike behaviour' the previous year when he went to the assistance of the fallen Welsh captain, Colin Charvis, after Charvis was tackled and injured during a Test match between Wales and the All Blacks. While the game continued, the dread-locked Umaga went to Charvis' aid. Others who have been honoured with the Award are Arthur Ashe, Bobby Charlton, Martina Navratilova and Sergei Bubka. Umaga is the first New Zealander to receive the award.

1761 Marie Tussaud was born in Strasbourg, Germany. Some of her wax sculptures still survive. She died in London in 1850.

1912 A remarkable bust of Nefertiti, a 14th century Egyptian queen, was discovered at an archaeological site.

1953 David Ben-Gurion resigned as the first Premier of Israel. A Zionist guerilla in his youth, he studied Greek and Sanskrit in his later years to understand the Scriptures. He died in 1973.

1985 Robert Graves, the British poet, died aged 90. He wrote *Goodbye to All That*, deploring the carnage of war.

1995 Secret Women's Business: In a highly publicised case, the Australian Federal Court found the Aboriginal Affairs Minister failed to follow due process in the controversial South Australian Hindmarsh Island Bridge case. Local women fought the bridge's construction as it violated sacred ground where they performed tradtional ceremonies.

Black smoke pours from *USS California* on fire in Pearl Harbour, Oahu Island after the surprise attack by the Japanese which brought America into WW II.

8 DECEMBER

1991: Soviet Union Over

The Union of Soviet Socialist Republic (USSR), or Soviet Union, was dissolved with the founding of the Commonwealth of Independent States (CIS) in 1991. The leaders of the Russian, Ukrainian and Belarusian republics met in Belavezhskaya Pushcha, Belarus, to issue a declaration that the Soviet Union was dissolved and replaced by the CIS. Mikhail Gorbachev became president without a country since Boris Yeltsin was the elected President of Russia. The CIS replaced the fading USSR, which was founded in 1922 and manages the foreign and economic policies of the member nations: Armenia, Azerbaijan, Kazakhastan, Kyrgyzstan, Modova, Takikistan, Turkmenistan and Uzbekistan. Georgia chose not to join. It has been a difficult process for the separate countries to move slowly away from Communism to capitalism and deal with separatist rivalries and nationalist issues. *New Yorker* reports that Russia now has more billionaires than any other country in the world.

1997: Jenny Shipley

Shipley made history when she became the first female Prime Minister of New Zealand. She was born in Gore, New Zealand in 1952. She taught primary school before entering politics. Jenny Shipley made changes in transportation, welfare reform, women's affairs and public health. The Labour Party's Helen Clark defeated Shipley in 1999 and Shipley continued to head the centre-right National Party until she retired in 2001.

2004: Shania Twain

The Canadian singer's *Come on Over* became the best-selling selling country album ever in America, according to the Recording Industry Association of America. Twain was born on 28 August 1965, near Windsor, Ontario, with the birth name Eileen Edwards. Shania is an Ojibway Indian name translated as 'I'm on my way.'

1939 James Galway the talented flutist was born in Belfast, Northern Ireland. He started playing a penny-whistle as a child and is now one of the world's most popular flutists.

1976 The Eagles released their best selling album, Hotel California.

1980 John Lennon, the 40-year-old Beatle turned solo artist was shot and killed outside his flat in New York.

1995 The Chinese government enthroned a six-year old Panchen Lama, in place of the Dalai Lama's choice.

1998 Japanese scientists reported that they had cloned eight calves from one dead cow. This indicated that cloning could be as efficient as in-vitro fertilisation.

2001 Frances Holbertson a pioneering computer programmer on ENIAC died age 84. She helped write the programming languages COBOL and FORTRAN.

Canadian singer, Shania Twain, performs during a taping of the CBS Early Show in 2003, outside the CBS Studios, New York City.

9 DECEMBER

1934: Dame Judi Dench

The popular British actress was born in York. Dench started her career aged five, playing the role of a snail. She has played versatile roles from comedy television sketches and sit-coms to Shakespeare. She achieved her greatest fame in her mid 60s, playing a strong dignified woman in roles such as Jean in the BBC TV sitcom, *As Time Goes By*. Her movies include *Golden Eye*, *A Room with a View* and *Iris*. Dench won an Oscar for Best Supporting Actress for her role as Queen Elizabeth I in *Shakespeare in Love*. Her career spans more than four decades.

1991: Maastricht Treaty

The European Council began negotiations in the Dutch town of Maastricht for the Treaty on European Union. The signing of the treaty, in February 1992, was an important step toward the creation of the European Union. It went into effect two years later when 12 nations ratified it. The European Union grew from the Common Market and the European Economic Community. The goal of a Europe without frontiers has made slow progress because of ancient histories and ingrained nationalism. A common currency, the euro, was adopted in 2002 by most European nations, but not Britain.

1996: Mary Leakey

The British archaeologist and anthropologist died in Nairobi, aged 83. Louis, her husband made his important archaeological discoveries of early man between 1925-36 in East Africa. In 1947, as newly weds, Mary and Louis started searching the Olduvai Gorge, in Tanzania. They discovered the skull of *Proconsul africanus*, thought to be a distant ancestor of apes and early humans. In 1959, Mary discovered the skull of *Zinjanthropus boisie*, a pre-historic human-like creature, about 1.7 million years old. The Leakeys discovered *Homo habilis* and *Homo erectus*, who were known to have made implements. Mary continued her research after Louis died in 1972 and discovered the oldest evidence of the origins of man, in 1978: footprints proving that hominids walked upright 3.5 million years ago. Smoking cigars and searching for bone fragments, Mary remained active up until her peaceful death aged 83 in Nairobi. Their son, Richard, continued his parents' research and discovered an almost complete Homo erectus. He is in charge of Kenya's wildlife parks.

1916 Canada's 8km rail tunnel opened in the Selkirk Range, British Columbia. It took two years to blast.

1939 A dress that Judy Garland wore in The Wizard of Oz sold for a world record £199 500 at Christie's auction.

1960 Coronation Street was first aired on British television.

1987 The English cricket tour to Pakistan was nearly called off when a row broke out between Mike Gatting and a Pakistani umpire. If the game had been cancelled it would have been the first in the Tour's 111-year history.

1991 In what was termed 'improbable,' the underdog French tennis team won the Davis Cup for the first time in 59 years.

Actress Judi Dench attends the premiere of *Iris* December 2, 2001 at the Paris Theatre in New York City.

10 DECEMBER

1792: Captain Arthur Phillip

After serving as Governor for four difficult years, Phillip left the penal colony of New South Wales to return home to England. His powers as the colony's founding Governor were absolute. While he sought harmony with the Aboriginal people, he also believed in the superiority of the British way of life. When he left , Phillip took with him an Aboriginal, Bennelong, who had acted as an interpreter, and Yemmerrawannie. Bennelong enjoyed England because he spoke English and became quite a dandy. He returned to Australia in 1795. Sydney's Opera House stands on Bennelong Point, known as Tubowghule by the local Aboriginal people, where Bennelong lived in a brick hut built for him by Phillip.

1830: Emily Dickinson

One of America's great poets was born in Amherst, Massachusetts. Dickinson was practically unknown in her lifetime and only seven of her poems were published. She became a recluse in later life and only left her family home at dusk, when she would wander in her garden if no one were present. Emily's last words at age 55 were, 'I must go in for the fog is rising.' Her sister, Lavinia, discovered nearly 2000 poems that Emily had written on tiny scraps of paper or bound into small books.

1851: Melvil Dewey

The creator of the Dewey Decimal Classification system (DDC) for arranging non-fiction library books, was born at Adams Centre, New York. While working as a 21-year-old student in the Amherst, Massachusetts University Library, Dewey invented the DDC, beginning a new era in librarianship. He founded the first library school in New York in 1887. With his friend and fellow librarian Charles Cutter, Dewey founded the American Library Association. Dewey is also credited with inventing the first vertical office file. Dewey died aged 80 in 1931 in Highlands County, Florida. His DDC is still used worldwide, although larger libraries and research institutions use the Library of Congress System, based on an alphanumeric system.

1882 Tailoresses Union: Australia's first female union was formed five days after a successful strike by female employees against a clothing manufacturer in Melbourne.

1901 The first Nobel Prizes were awarded. Four institutions, three Swedish and one Norwegian, selected the laureates.

1904 Ivan Pavlov won a Nobel Prize for his work on the digestive processes and 'conditioned responses.'

1912 Alexis Carrel, the French scientist, won a Nobel Prize for his work on sewing blood vessels together and for keeping organs alive outside the body, which opened up the possibility of human transplants.

1922 Niels Bohr, the Danish physicist, was awarded the Nobel Prize for using quantum physics to explain the atom's internal structure.

Emily Elizabeth Dickinson (1830-1886) withdrew herself at the age of 23 from all social contacts and lived an intensely secluded life, writing over 1000 poems.

11 DECEMBER

1895: George Whitehouse

The renowned engineer arrived in Mombassa, East Africa, to start building a railway line known as the 'Lunatic Express.' Its purpose was to make the British Protectorate of Uganda easier to reach from the coast. Overland trips by foot were dangerous because of hostile tribes, wild animals and disease. Construction on the Lunatic Express began in 1896, using 13 000 imported Indian labourers, many of whom died from tropical diseases. Man-eating lions also ate dozens of workers. The Lunatic Express was laid out to reach Lake Victoria, some 1000km away. It climbed 1150m, crossed the Equator, lost 600m altitude at the Rift Valley, climbed out again and crossed a 160km swamp. Three years into the project, the workers reached a pleasant watering spot called Nyrobi. Whitehouse decided that this would be the main staging area for the Rift Valley construction portion. In 1901 the track was dedicated. Many of the original workers made their home in what became Nairobi, making it an instant multi-ethnic city. The Lunatic Express helped create modern Kenya.

1999: Sistine Chapel

The pride of the Vatican was re-opened after twenty years of restoration work. The chapel was built between 1475-83 and is best known for the exquisite ceiling frescoes painted by Michelangelo. Michelangelo finished them in 1512, but the true colour of the works was hidden beneath a layer of dust over hundreds of years. Now experts believe the works are seen the way the artist intended them, with colour that should last decades. Some of the renovations took twice as long to clean as they did to paint.

2004: Arthur Lydiard

New Zealand's most successful athletics coach died aged 84, in Texas. He was on a lecture tour on training methods. Five of his protégées competed in the 1960 Rome Olympics. Within one hour Peter Snell set an Olympic record and won the gold for the 800m and Murray Halberg won gold in the 5000m. In the 1964 Tokyo Olympics, protégées Peter Snell and John Davies won medals.

1866 The first Transatlantic Ocean yacht race was held, won by *Henrietta*. The boats had set sail from Plymouth, England on 6 September.

1936 Britain's Edward VIII abdicated and his brother became King George VI. Edward had ascended the throne on 20 January, but was never crowned.

1978 Massive demonstrations took place in Tehran, Iran against the Shah. In Isfahan 40 people were killed and 60 wounded.

1986 British Church leaders were incensed over a radio campaign against AIDS-HIV that urged people to 'Play It Safe.' The leaders said the message promoted promiscuity.

1993 The United Nations approved the creation of a Commissioner for Human Rights to respond quickly to world-wide crises, after 45 years of discussion.

2003 Religious garments banned: A French panel concluded that the country should outlaw blatant religious identifiers in public schools. Islamic veils, Jewish skull caps and Christian crucifixes were identified as unwelcome in the classroom. The ban became law in 2004 when the French National Assembly voted overwhelmingly in its favour.

Legendary New Zealand athletics coach Arthur Lydiard of New Zealand poses in the UK in the early 1990s. Lydiard coached Peter Snell to an 800 and 1500 metres double at the Rome Olympic Games in 1960.

12 DECEMBER

1995: Andrew Olle

One of Australia's most popular radio journalists died unexpectedly from a brain tumour in Sydney. The 47-year-old radio and TV journalist, programmer and broadcaster was born in 1947. He joined the ABC in Brisbane and spent the next 27 years as a journalist. His integrity was such that no one knew his political views. His interviews with the powerful or the downtrodden were conducted with equal professionalism and sincerity. The Andrew Olle Media Lecture was established in his memory and has become a significant media industry forum.

2003: J M Coetzee

The South African born writer received the Nobel Prize for Literature. Coetzee graduated from the University of Cape Town in 1961. He moved to England and then taught in America, returning home to teach English Literature at the University of Cape Town. In 2002, he immigrated to Adelaide, Australia, where he lives. He has won the Man Booker Prize twice. His writing addresses South Africa's issues of post apartheid, imperialism and suffering. Some of his works include *In the Heart of the Country, The Life and Times of Michael K* and *Disgrace*. Coetzee dedicated his Nobel Prize to his mother, wishing she could have lived to see him win.

2003: Layne Beachley

Australia's greatest female professional surfer won her sixth consecutive world title, something no man or woman has ever done. 'Beach' was born in 1972 and calls Manly, New South Wales, home. Beachley was adopted as a child and grew up as a strong young woman, playing soccer, tennis and practically living in the water. At age 16 she turned professional and by age 20 she was ranked sixth in the world. Beachley founded the Layne Beachley Aim for the Stars Foundation, which gives moral and financial support to women with aspirations of greatness. As a pro surfer, she promotes women's surfing worldwide. She divides her time between Australia and Hawaii.

Four times ASP World Champion, Australia's Layne Beachley, clinches the 2002 Roxy Pro title in Hossegor, France.

1917 Australian Prime Minister Billy Hughes established the Commonwealth Police Force, after being hit with an egg and the Queensland Government refusing to become involved.

1930 Norman and Clarence Burt opened the first of that unique Australian institution, the milk bar, in Sydney.

1968 Tallulah Bankhead, the tempestuous American stage and movie actress died. Her major successes were in *The Little Foxes* on stage and *Hitchcock's Lifeboat* on screen.

1977 Lady Spencer-Churchill, the beloved widow of Sir Winston Churchill, died aged 92. Clementine was 'the most fortunate and joyous event …in the whole of my life,' Churchill said.

1999 The Princess Royal, Anne, only daughter of Queen Elizabeth II and Philip, the Duke of Edinburgh, married for the second time.

13 DECEMBER

1871: Emily Carr

The Canadian artist and writer was born and raised in Victoria, British Columbia. She studied in San Francisco, London and Paris before returning to Vancouver. Carr's portraits of indigenous people and west coast landscapes established her as one of Canada's best-known painters, but her greatest fame came in her late fifties. She painted mainly forest scenes, landscapes and native images. As her health deteriorated and she became bedridden, she turned to writing books, including: *The Book of Small* and *The House of All Sorts. Klee Wyck* won the Governor General's Award in 1941. Carr died in 1945, but her Victoria home is now open to the public and an art school has been established in her name.

1955: Dame Edna Everage

The Dame of stage and screen (Barry Humphries) made her first appearance. 'Hello Possums' is her trademark opening line. Claiming to be the 'most talented and gifted woman in the world,' the outrageous pink haired, heavily made up Dame Edna denies being a fictional character or 'just a drag queen.' She claims to have been born in Melbourne, Australia with a precious gift: 'Dame Nature stooped over my cot and gave me the ability to laugh at the misfortunes of others.' Her manager and alter ego, Barry Humphries, is an Australian writer, comedian, artist, actor and film producer, who was born in Melbourne in 1934. His Dame Edna has become one of Australia's iconic characters on television and stage. Dame Edna is modelled in wax at Madame Tussaud's Wax Museum in London. Humphries is also Sir Les Patterson, Australia's cultural ambassador.

1998: Kelly Slater

The surfer won his sixth world surfing title and announced his retirement from the gruelling professional surfing circuit. He had competed selectively, since eclipsing Newcastle, Australia's Mark Richard's four world titles. Born in 1972 in Cocoa Beach Florida, he first rode a surfboard at the age of five. Turning professional at 18, Slater won the $100 000 Body Glove Surf Bout contest in 1990. Slater became known as 'the Michael Jordan of Surfing.' He has won more surfing titles than anyone. Regarded by many as the greatest surfer, Slater was inducted into the International Surfing Hall of Fame in 2002. He has appeared in surfing videos and has acted in the hit TV series *Baywatch*. *People* magazine ranked him as one its Fifty Most Beautiful People in 1991. Slater is also a writer, businessman, musician and is the subject of a video game.

1642 Captain Abel Janszoon Tasman of the Dutch East India Company first sighted New Zealand and noted it in his journal. A bloody encounter with indigenous Maoris prevented his landing.

1912 Marcus Thompson, the 'father of modern roller coasters', built the Scenic Railway at St. Kilda's Luna Park in Victoria. It is probably the world's oldest continually operating roller coaster.

1922 Christopher Plummer, the stage and screen actor, was born in Toronto, Canada. He has appeared in more than 80 movies, including the lead in *The Sound of Music*.

1947 The United Nations appointed Australia as trustee for Papua-New Guinea, following World War II.

2003 Iraqi President Saddam Hussein was found hiding in an underground hideout in Tikrit. No shots were fired and he was taken into custody.

Celebrity Dame Edna attends the taping of 'Hollywood Squares' at the CBS Television City Studios in Hollywood, California, in 2003.

14 DECEMBER

1991: Mt Cook Decapitated

The summit of New Zealand's picturesque Mt Cook collapsed, displacing an estimated 10 million cubic metres of snow, ice and rock. The top of the 3000 m high mountain is now an exposed ice ridge. The Maori name for the mountain is Aoraki, meaning cloud piercer. It was named in honour of Captain James Cook in 1851. The first known people to climb the mountain were New Zealand's George Graham, Jack Clark and Tom Fyfe, in 1894. The first woman to reach the summit was an Australian nurse, Freda Du Faur in 1910. The mountain has claimed more than 200 lives. The surrounding area is a World Heritage Site and is often used as a backdrop in movies, such as Peter Jackson's *Lord of the Rings: The Fellowship of the Ring*.

1994: Three Gorges Dam

Chinese Premier Li Ping announced the planned construction of the controversial Three Gorges Dam, the biggest project undertaken by China since the Great Wall. When completed, in 2009, Three Gorges will be the world's largest hydroelectric dam. Those in favour of the dam believe it will prevent devastating and recurring flooding of the Yangtze River, provide more hydroelectricity than fifteen coal-burning power stations combined and provide more efficient forms of shipping. It will allow freighters and cargo boats to travel directly within the nation's interior instead of travelling around the periphery. Those opposed to the project call it the most socially and environmentally destructive project in history. More than 100 towns will be submerged, forcing 1.2 million residents to resettle. The dam will permanently alter and destroy delicate ecosystems. The project is currently facing massive corruption problems, spiralling costs, technological problems and resettlement difficulties.

2003: Teatro La Fenice

Venice's famed opera house was re-opened to the public. In 1996 the theatre burned down for the third time since its inauguration in 1792. Italian investigators determined the cause was arson, resulting from a dispute between two electrical contractors. They were sentenced to six and seven years prison. Bidding disputes between rival contracting companies delayed the Teatro's reconstruction for seven years. La Fenice, appropriately, means the Phoenix rising from the flames. It is one of the world's most beautiful opera houses. *La Traviata* and *Rigoletto* were first performed there.

1918 Women in Great Britain were allowed to vote and to stand as candidates for Parliament for the first time. The first to win a seat was Senn Fein's Countess Markievicz, who was in prison.

1920 The British House of Lords approved the Government of Ireland Act, which divided Ireland into two separate regions, each with its own parliament and administration.

1947 Stanley Baldwin, three times British Prime Minister, died.

1973 John Paul Getty III, the grandson of one of the world's richest men, was released after being held hostage for six months. A ransom of $750 000 was paid. As proof of his capture, his ear was cut off and sent to his grandfather.

1987 Australian cricketer Allan Border scored a double-century against New Zealand and became cricket's highest scorer.

John Paul Getty III survived a horrific kidnap ordeal as a teenager, losing one of his ears in the process. When he married a German artist he was disinherited for violating a clause in his grandfather's will that required heirs to marry only after the age of 26. A mixture of prescription drugs, taken in 1980, rendered him comatose for six weeks and left him paralysed and visually impaired.

15 DECEMBER

1859: Lazarus Zamenhof
The creator of Esperanto was born in Bialystok, near the borders of Poland, Lithuania and Belarus. He was exposed to many languages as a child, which made him realise the need for an international tongue. Esperanto means 'He Who Hopes.' Zamenhof died in 1917. The organisation the International Society of Friendship and Good Will continues his work.

1939: Gone With The Wind
One of the most acclaimed American movies of all time premiered in Atlanta, Georgia. Producer, David Selznick, and director, Victor Fleming, worried at how the movie would be received in the American South, as it was based on Margaret Mitchell's sweeping novel of the Civil War era and portrayed the burning of Atlanta. The audience, however, was thrilled and Mitchell gave a speech at its conclusion. Praise was given to the perfect casting of English actress Vivien Leigh as Scarlett O'Hara and Clark Gable as Rhett Butler. *Gone with the Wind* also stars box office draws Leslie Howard and Olivia de Havilland. Hattie McDaniel, who played the role of Scarlett's maid, was the first African-American to receive an Oscar. It is the story of the headstrong Scarlett, her three marriages and her determination to keep the family plantation, Tara, despite the Civil War. Mitchell won a Pulitzer Prize in 1936 for this, her only novel. She died aged 49 in Atlanta in a pedestrian accident.

1944: Glenn Miller
The 40-year-old band leader and two of his band members disappeared in heavy fog over the English Channel while on their way to France to entertain American troops. His swing music was extremely popular before and during World War II. He played trombone and was the arranger for his band. His signature hits included 'In the Mood' and 'String of Pearls'. More than four decades later, a Royal Air Force bomber crew said that they had seen his single engine plane go down. Bombs dumped by the Royal Air Force probably hit the plane.

1593 Dutch wind power: A patent was granted in the Netherlands for a windmill with a crankshaft.

1840 Napoleon Bonaparte's remains were interred in Paris's Les Invalides having been brought from St Helena, where he had died.

1856 France's Pierre Maigre advertised a hot air balloon ascent in Sydney's Domain. 15 000 spectators turned out. When the balloon failed to work, chaos ensued, leaving a dead child and the balloon torn to shreds.

1962 Charles Laughton, British stage and screen actor died. He starred in *Mutiny on the Bounty* and was known for his stage readings of GB Shaw.

1966 Walt Disney died, aged 65. The American was a film producer, animator and theme park developer. His characters, Mickey Mouse and Donald Duck, are loved by children worldwide.

The American trombonist and band-leader, Glenn Miller (1904-1944), who disappeared when a small aircraft he was a passenger in went down over the English Channel.

16 DECEMBER

1917: Arthur C Clarke

The influential visionary writer was born in Minehead, England. He made a telescope as a child to pursue his fascination with stars and space. An expert in aeronautics and astronautics, he was highly regarded in the scientific community even though he was not formally educated in astronomy. His books accurately predicted satellites and radio transmissions from space. His science fiction includes *2001: A Space Odyssey, The Nine Billion Names of God* and *Islands in the Sky,* plus many works of non-fiction about space travel. He wrote, 'Any sufficiently advanced technology is indistinguishable from magic.'

1921: Camille Saint-Saens

The French composer, pianist, organist and a leader in French music for over six decades, died aged 86, in Algiers. He began composing at age six and performed publicly at age ten. After his first symphony premiered in 1853, composer Charles Gounod wrote to Saint-Saens, saying that he 'had the obligation to be a great master.' He wrote 15 operas, including *Samson and Delilah, Danse Macabre* and the popular *Carnival of the Animals* for children. His lifetime coincided with the increased popularity of opera in France. In 1865, Paris' magnificent opera house opened, called simply Opéra, designed by Charles Garnier.

2004: Millau Bridge

The world's tallest bridge was opened in Millau, France by President Jacques Chirac. Lord Norman Foster, the British architect somehow seemed to make the steel structure float, by using white cables that disappear against the sky. Stretching over 2460m through the mountains of France, the Viaduc de Millau took over three years to complete. The engineering wonder is over 270m above ground, making it taller than the Paris Eiffel Tower.

2004: David Blunkett

Britain's Home Secretary, the third-most powerful politician in Britain, resigned because of a visa impropriety. He helped his former lover's nanny fast track a work and tourist visa. While claiming no recollection of the alleged impropriety, the Minister acknowledged that he was under enormous pressure because his former lover was claiming that a baby she was pregnant with, which he had believed was his, was in fact her husband's. The case was made sordid because his former lover, a magazine publisher, had leaked the story. Blunkett had been widely admired in Britain because he had been blind since birth.

1948 The *HMAS Sydney*, Australia's first aircraft carrier, was commissioned.

1949 Achmad Sukarno was elected Indonesia's first president after the Netherlands relinquished its sovereignty. A long and bloody battle for independence, that had started after the defeat of the occupying Japanese and the return of Dutch colonial power in 1945, ended.

1969 The British House of Commons voted 343:185 to abolish the death penalty.

1987 Sicily attempted to tackle its organised crime problem and convicted 338 people, the largest Mafia trial ever.

1997 In Japan 700 young television viewers experienced seizures and nausea while watching a brightly animated and flashing cartoon show.

The first of twenty-thousand people arrive at the world's tallest bridge, the Milau Bridge.

17 DECEMBER

1874: W L Mackenzie King

Canada's Prime Minister for 21 years was born in Berlin (now Kitchener), Ontario. He served the longest term of any Prime Minister in the English-speaking world. First elected in 1921, he was forced to resign in 1926 over allegations of 'wild parties' held by his Liberal colleagues during Prohibition in the national capital, Ottawa. There were also Customs Department irregularities involving shipments of alcohol to America, which was 'dry.' King's government might have survived except his party was in a minority-coalition in Parliament. Later King was re-elected and saw Canada through the turbulence of the World War II. He cooperated closely with the UK's Prime Minister Winston Churchill and American President Franklin Roosevelt. He died in Kingsmere, Quebec, in July 1950, two years after retiring from office.

1903: Kitty Hawk

The dream of mankind to fly like a bird was realised when the first successfully observed and recorded heavier-than-air machine flew at Kitty Hawk, North Carolina. Wilbur and Orville Wright, inventors since childhood, experimented with unmanned gliders for years. From 1900-1902 they launched a series of manned gliders and progressed to a fabric-covered biplane with a wooden frame. A 12hp, water-cooled engine connected to two contra-rotating propellers powered the aircraft. By the historic day's end, both had flown the machine. Orville flew the biplane for 12-seconds, followed by Wilbur's one-minute flight. They continued to build and test better airplanes and in 1905, Wilbur flew an impressive 38km in thirty minutes, at an altitude of around three metres. When Wilbur died, seven years later, Orville gave up building planes.

1989: The Simpsons

One of the funniest and most popular shows on television premiered. Matt Groening, *The Simpsons*' creator, loosely based the animated show on characters in his own life in Portland Oregon. Groening was born in 1954 and doodled his way through school. His first success was a comic strip, *Life in Hell*. *The Simpsons* is enjoyed in more than 70 different countries and is the longest running prime-time animated series in history, winning over 30 Emmy awards. The characters are named after the members of Groenings' real-life family.

1919 Pierre Renoir, the French Impressionist artist died, aged 78. When arthritis crippled him, he used a paintbrush strapped to his hand.

1956 The New York Supreme Court ruled that 12m yachts could be used in the America's Cup Race. This meant the end of the J-Sloop era.

1967 Harold Holt, the Australian Prime Minister disappeared while swimming at Portsea, Victoria. Despite rumours of submarines and sharks, he presumably drowned.

1974 Harrods of London, the exclusive department store, was bombed. A caller gave ten minutes warning for the store's evacuation but six people died and 75 were injured. It was believed to be the work of the Irish Republican Army.

1986 Medical history was made when a patient received the first lung, heart and liver transplant at Papworth Hospital, Cambridge, England.

1996 Sun Yaoting, the last Chinese Imperial eunuch died, aged 93. Eunuchs were entrusted with caring for the Emperor's family, including food-tasting.

Matt Groening, the cartoonist and creator of 'The Simpsons' in 1992, with a cardboard cutout of Bart Simpson.

18 DECEMBER

1642: First Bloody Contact

The first recorded contact took place between Maoris and Europeans in New Zealand. Two Dutch ships, the Heemskerck and Zeehaen, under the command of Captain Abel Janszoon Tasman, anchored in Golden Bay on the northwest tip of the South Island. The Maori paddled out in two canoes, called out and blew a war trumpet. Tasman ordered a trumpeter to play in response. The next day, a group of canoes paddled out to the two ships, but the Maori rammed a rowboat and killed four sailors. When more canoes approached the ships the Dutch shot and killed at least one Maori. Tasman called the place Murderers' Bay. Tasman's name was later given to the sea between Australia and New Zealand and the Australian state, Tasmania.

1872: Australian Opals

The world-renowned gemstones were first discovered at Listowel Downs, in Queensland. A larger opal field was later discovered at Coober Pedy, New South Wales. Tourists flock to the area to turn over mine tailings in hopes of finding some gemstones. Coober Pedy is also a most unusual towns where everyone lives underground to escape the blistering heat. A 19th century author created a superstition that opals bring bad luck, but that was no more realistic than the advertising slogan that 'a diamond is forever.' Australia is also home to the world's largest diamond mine, the Western Australian Argyle mine, where rare, pink diamonds are mined.

1946: Steven Spielberg

One of the world's famous and wealthiest movie directors was born in Cincinnati, Ohio. He began making movies when he was in primary school, experimenting with short films. He won his first prize, aged 13, for a short war film *Escape to Nowhere*. Spielberg's first major blockbuster was *Jaws*. It was so realistic that viewers were terrified to go near the ocean. In 1977, Spielberg won the Best Director's Oscar for *Close Encounters of the Third Kind*. Other classics are *Star Wars*, *Raiders of the Lost Ark*, *Indiana Jones and the Temple of Doom*, *ET*, *Poltergeist*, *Gremlins*, *Back to the Future*, *The Colour Purple*, *Jurassic Park*, *Schindler's List*, *Saving Private Ryan* and *War of the Worlds*.

1737 Antonio Stradivari, history's most renowned violin maker, died aged 93 in Cremona Italy. His violins sell for millions of dollars.

1890 Edwin H Armstrong, the developer of FM radio, was born in New York. His inventions and developments form the backbone of radio communications as we know it. His discovery of frequency modulation eliminated radio static and is the basis of FM radio.

1892 Sir Richard Owen, the English scientist, , who created the word 'dinosaur' (terrible reptile) died. He was an anatomist and paleontologist and created many other words used in anatomy and evolutionary biology.

1970 Despite Roman Catholic Church opposition, divorce law went into effect in Italy.

1975 George and Kathy Lutz moved into a house in Amityville, New York and four weeks later moved out because the claimed it was haunted by a poltergeist and oozed slime. Their tales spawned the movie, *The Amityville Horror*.

Director Steven Spielberg attends the 15th Annual Glamour 'Women of the Year' Awards at the American Museum of Natural History, in New York City in 2004 .

19 DECEMBER

1848: Emily Bronte

The British author died, aged 30, from tuberculosis. She was largely unappreciated during her brief life, but is now acknowledged as one of England's greatest 19th century poets. Born in 1818, in Yorkshire she was one of six children of an Anglican clergyman. Her mother died, soon followed by Emily's two oldest sisters Maria and Elizabeth, all from tuberculosis. Emily and her surviving sisters, Charlotte and Anne, enjoyed writing and were extremely close. *Wuthering Heights* was the only book Emily published in her lifetime. It was only recognised as a masterpiece after her death. Critics insisted a man must have written it, because 'decent' women were incapable of writing passionate stories of love and revenge. The book reflects the tragedy of Emily's own life. She fell ill with tuberculosis after her brother's funeral. Anne died of tuberculosis the following year and Charlotte later died during pregnancy.

1987: Garry Kasparov

The 24-year-old chess player beat Anatoly Karpov in Seville, Spain to retain his title as World Champion. Born in Baku, Azerbaijan, Kasparov's chess skills attracted attention when he was a small child and he trained at Mikhail Botvinnik's Chess School. In 1978, Kasparov won the Sokolsky Memorial Tournament and became a master. He set his sights on the Chess World Championship and first won in 1985. At 22, he was the youngest world champion. He reigned until 2000. He established the Grandmasters Association in 1987. In 1996 he played IBM's Deep Blue computer and won 4:6, but lost the next year. Deep Blue was able to evaluate 200 million chess positions per second. Kasparov created *Advanced Chess*, a new computer chess game. In 2003, Kasparov played the X3D Fritz computer and drew. He retired in 2005.

2004: Jamie O'Brien

The Hawaiian wildcard entrant became the youngest surfer to win the Pipeline Masters, the longest running and one of the most prestigious surfing contests in the world. The men's-only surf competition is held annually in December at Pipeline Beach, Oahu, Hawaii, renowned for having the best tubing waves, or 'tubes'. Nobody was more surprised than 21-year-old O'Brien, who had always dreamed of winning.

1906 Burrinjuck and Murrumbidgee: Legislation was passed for the construction of an enormous irrigation scheme that would help create a great food growing area on the western plains of New South Wales.

1907 The world's first non-contributory invalid pension was passed by the New South Wales Parliament to go into effect 1 January 1908.

1946 War broke out in Indo-China when Ho Cho Minh attacked the French. This developed into the protracted Vietnam War.

1997 Janet Jagon was sworn in as Guyana's first female President.

1999 Macau ceased to be a Portuguese territory at midnight and reverted to Chinese administration.

Hawaiian wildcard entrant Jamie O'Brien surfs en route to clinching his maiden Rip Curl Pro Pipeline Masters title on December 19, 2004. O'Brien beat Triple Crown winner Sunny Garcia to pocket US$30,000 in prize money.

20 DECEMBER

1954: James Hilton

The British novelist, also known as Glen Trevor, died aged 54 in Long Beach, California. He is best remembered for his fictitious adventure story *Lost Horizon* written in 1933, after a visit to the rugged mountains of Pakistan on the borders of Kashmir, Afghanistan and China. *Lost Horizon* was set in a Tibetan monastery called 'Shangri La' where everyone lived in peace and enjoyed extended youth. It was made into a highly successful movie. Hilton also wrote *Goodbye Mr. Chips*, a novella about a schoolteacher, which also became a popular movie. He won an Oscar for his screenplay, *Mrs Miniver*. His birthplace, Leigh in Manchester, has honoured him with a plaque.

1969: Janis Joplin

The energetic blues singer was described in the usually staid *New York Times* as having given an 'excellent performance before a near-capacity crowd at Madison Square Garden last night.' The reviewer described her meteoric career over the previous two years, from solo performer to her stint with various bands including the six-member Big Brother and the Holding Company, the Kozmic Blues Band and the Full Tilt Boogie Band. In 1969 she was at the height of her career, after nine years of a roller-coaster life, intense performing, touring and difficult relationships. Among Joplin's best-known songs are 'Mercedes Benz', 'Bobby McGee' and 'Piece of My Heart.' Her masterpiece album, *Pearl*, was released in 1971 and topped the charts for nine weeks. She did not see its successful release, as she died of a drug overdose on 4 October 1970, aged 27, in Hollywood.

2004: Northern Ireland Heist

One of the world's biggest bank robberies took place in Belfast, Northern Ireland. About twenty armed robbers pulled off the well-organised heist at the Northern Bank (NB). The families of two bank executives were held at gunpoint for over 24 hours, while the executives were forced to help the robbers clean out about £26.5 million from the vaults. The families were later released unharmed. After the robbery, the bank took several weeks to withdraw almost all of its notes and replace them with banknotes of different colours hoping to make the stolen money useless. The NB acknowledged that the stolen money could still be spent. Police accused the Irish Republican Army (IRA), but the IRA denies any involvement. Forty-five detectives were assigned to the investigation. In February 2005 a number of arrests were made and some money recovered

1791 Thomas Baillairge was born in Quebec City, the third generation architect in his family. He designed many of Canada's most famous churches, including Notre Dame Cathedral. He died in 1859.

1886 Hazel H Wightman, tennis player, was born in Healdsburg, California. In a long tennis career, she won many American singles and doubles titles. She donated the Wightman Cup that is contested by the America and Britain.

1983 Bill Brandt, the pioneering English photographer died, aged 79. His work incorporated mystery and drama. His 1970 photographic exhibition was the first to ever receive English Arts Council support.

1985 American Poet Laureate: A bill was signed into law creating the post. The first was Robert Penn Warren in 1986.

1998 America's President Bill Clinton was impeached by the American House of representatives over the Monica Lewinsky affair. The Senate acquitted him.

A group of children playing leap frog in the street in a typical street life photo by Bill Brandt. Originally published in *Picture Post*, 1950.

21 DECEMBER

1898: Marie and Pierre Curie

The collaborative couple discovered radium. Together, they also discovered and isolated polonium, named after Marie's beloved homeland Poland. In 1903, the pair shared the Nobel Prize for Physics. Their work led to the use of X-rays in medicine and the splitting the atom. Pierre was French and they met at the Sorbonne University. Pierre never thought he would marry, because he needed a wife as brilliant as himself to be happy. After Pierre died in a pedestrian accident, Marie received the Nobel Prize for Chemistry in 1911. She was the first person to be awarded two Nobel Prizes. However, because she was a woman, she failed to be elected to the French Academy of Science. Four members of the Curie family won Nobel Prizes and shaped the field of nuclear physics. Their daughter, Irene and her husband, Frédéric Joliot, both staunch socialists and anti-fascists, shared the Nobel Prize for Chemistry in 1935. Marie, and later Irene, died of leukaemia, most likely from radiation exposure.

1940: Frank Zappa

The iconoclastic musician of the 1960s was born in Baltimore, Maryland. As a child, Zappa played drums and guitar. After dropping out of college he formed The Mothers of Invention whose lyrics outraged critics. The prolific musician and outspoken advocate of creative freedom recorded more than sixty albums. Zappa's outrageous sense of humour combined with his skill at composing and producing made him an icon. Zappa's rare mastering of classical music techniques, along with his deviant satirical sense of humour were a strange combination and appealed to a worldwide audience. Zappa and his wife Gail had five children, Moon Unit, Dweezil, Ahmet, Rodan and Diva. In 1993 Zappa died aged 52 from cancer in Los Angeles. In 1994 an asteroid was named *Zappafrank* in his honour and he was inducted into the Rock and Roll Hall of Fame in 1995.

1988: Pan Am Flight 103

An explosion in the cargo bay brought down Pan American's Flight 103 over Lockerbie, Scotland. The bomb killed all 259 passengers and crew and another 11 people on the ground. In the protracted investigations it was discovered that a bomb had been concealed in a cassette player and that government agencies and the airline had known that Flight 103 was possibly a target. Security procedures at airports were tightened after this incident and Pan American Airlines collapsed.

1894 South Australia was the first Australian state and one of the first places in the world, to grant women the right to vote.

1964 New Zealander Trevor Norton harpooned the last whale killed from a New Zealand ship in New Zealand waters.

1976 Rubin 'Hurricane' Carter was convicted of murdering three people, for a second time. His memoir was read by a student activist and attorney who fought for his release. Bob Dylan created interest in his plight with a hit song and a motion picture was made in 1999 starring Denzel Washington. He was released from prison in 1985.

1996 Laughing Bird Caye was inscribed as a World Heritage Site. It is off the coast of Belize in a chain of islands. The Caye takes its name from the Laughing Gull (Laurus articilla).

Studio portrait of American rock and roll musician Frank Zappa in 1990.

22 DECEMBER

1938: The Coelancath

A fish that had been assumed to be extinct for about 70 million years was 're-discovered' in the Indian Ocean off the east coast of South Africa. It is a large, lobe-finned fish that the fossil record shows was abundant 350 million years ago. Fishermen caught the 57kg, 1½ m-long fish and brought it to shore. It had blue scales, a paddle-like tail and bulging blue eyes. LB Smith, an ichthyologist, identified it. Fourteen years later, more specimens were discovered at their breeding ground, Comoros. Brown Coelancath were also found 9600km away, near Indonesia. Further study has revealed that the fish are nocturnal and that their fins are bones, which are flexible like elbows. Attempts to capture them and keep them in captivity for research have failed.

1944: Anthony McAuliffe,

The 101st US Airborne Division Acting Commander was given two hours to surrender to the Germans. The Germans had moved eight armoured divisions, under cover of rain, along a 120 km front in the Ardennes Hills of southern Belgium and Luxembourg. McAuliffe's famous one word reply was: 'Nuts'. The Allies held their ground and the Battle of the Bulge turned in the Allies' favour when General George S Patton rushed his 3rd Army in. The weather cleared in late December and Allied aircraft bombed German forces and supply lines to re-establish their original line. It was the largest land battle fought by Americans, involving 500 000 troops, plus 55 000 Britons, against 600 000 Germans. The six-week battle took an enormous toll—19 000 American dead and 61 000 wounded. The Germans lost 120 000.

1988: Chico Mendes

The environmental activist was murdered while attempting to halt the destruction of the Brazilian rainforest. Mendes was born in Northwestern Brazil in 1944. His family had worked for generations as rubber tappers. After cattle ranchers bought up the forests in the 1960s, clearing vast tracts for grazing land, Mendes led a group of non-violent activists to raise awareness about the rainforest's dilemma. Mendes' murder made international news. Two ranchers were found guilty. Mendes received awards from the United Nations and the Better World Society. The area where he lived and died was named a reserve in his honour. The destruction of Brazil's, and most of the world's, precious rainforests continues today and indigenous peoples are being forcefully evicted from the forests that have nurtured them for tens of thousands of years.

1907 Dame 'Peggy' Ashcroft was born in Croydon, England. She played more than 100 principal roles, ranging from comedy to tragedy. A theatre in London was named after her. She died in 1991.

1949 Twins Maurice and Robin Gibb were born on the Isle of Wight, England. With their brother Barry, they formed the hugely popular band the Bee Gees. The family moved to Australia in 1962, where they launched their first band, with songs such as 'How Deep Is Your Love?' and 'How Can You Mend a Broken Heart?'

1989 Nicolae Ceausescu, Romania's Communist dictator' was arrested as he tried to flee the capital, Bucharest, by helicopter. He and his wife were executed by firing squad on Christmas Day.

Brazilian activist and ecologist Chico Mendes, who was assassinated in his house in Xapuri, near the Amazon forest.

23 DECEMBER

1947: The Transistor

The vital component of virtually every modern electronic device was invented. It replaced the vacuum tube, which just a year previously had been heralded as an electronic breakthrough for use in calculators and computers. The transistor, a solid-state device, launched a revolution in communications and electronics. It was much more compact, generated less heat and required a lot less power than a vacuum tube. Three physicists from Bell Laboratories shared the Nobel Prize in Physics in 1956 for this work; John Bardeen, Walter Brattain and William Shockley. Bardeen received another Nobel Prize for Physics in 1972 for a fundamental theory of conventional conductivity. Bardeen is the only person to win two Nobel Prizes in Physics.

1956: Allied Troops Leave Suez

Egyptians poured onto the streets of Port Said to celebrate the withdrawal of British and French forces from Egypt. Their armed occupation of the region followed President Abdel Nasser's nationalisation of the Suez Canal. Shouting 'Long Live Nasser' the demonstrators burned British and French flags as the Allied forces withdrew to be replaced by a United Nations Emergency Force. The Suez crisis began in July 1956 when Nasser nationalised the Canal and blockaded the Straits of Tiran—Israel's main outlet into the Red Sea. Britain and France joined Israel to take control of Suez, although this alliance was denied for years. American President Eisenhower and the United Nations feared the Soviet Union would benefit from the crisis to gain influence in the Middle East.

1970: Catriona LeMay Doan

'The fastest woman on ice' was born in Sasskatoon, Sasskatchewan. The Olympic speed skater broke the 500m world record eight times. LeMay Doan became the first woman to break the barrier record of 38 seconds for the 500m. She won the World Cup three times and the 1000m once. In 1998 and again in 2001, she was named the Canadian Female Athlete of the Year. After 23 years of competitive skating, LeMay Doan announced her retirement in 2003.

British soldiers wish good luck to Danish United Nations soldiers as they withdraw from Egypt.

1601 When British invaders routed Irish forces near Kinsdale, it cleared the way for British settlement of Northern Ireland.

1861 The first horse-carriage service began in metropolitan Sydney.

1986 Voyager The experimental glider-like airplane completed a successful circumnavigation of the world, using just one load of fuel. It took slightly more than nine days.

2000 Victor Borge, the Danish comedian, died, aged 91. He delighted audiences with his classical music, punctuation routines.

2003 Mad cows in America: the first case of 'mad cow disease' was announced in Washington State.

24 DECEMBER

1971: Ricky Martin

The global teen sensation was born Enrique Martin in San Juan, Puerto Rico. Martin began appearing in TV commercials when he was six-years-old. He joined the teenage boy band sensation *Menudo* and toured with them for five years before moving to New York. He released his solo album *Ricky Martin* in 1988. He went on to perform on stage and television and was Hercules' voice in Disney's Spanish version of the animated movie. The debut English single of 'Livin' La Vida Loca' was a smash hit. Martin's face on *Time* magazine is credited with helping to bring Latin music into the American mainstream.

1945: Lemmy

The lead singer of Motorhead was born Ian Fraser Kilmister, in Staffordshire England. He joined his first band in 1964, was a roadie for Jimi Hendrix, then joined Hawkwind as bassist in 1971. He was kicked out of the band four years later and formed Motorhead, which became a major influence in heavy metal music worldwide. With Lemmy (singer/bassist), Phil Taylor (drums) and Eddie Clarke (guitar) the band's first release took England by storm in 1977. Thrashing out hits long before the Sex Pistols came along, Motorhead had long hair, leather jackets and a loud aggressive sound that personified 'heavy metal music'. With songs like 'Ace of Spades' Motorhead became notorious with fans worldwide. More than three decades later, Motorhead continues raging, putting on intense performances and playing sold out shows.

1997: Carlos the Jackal,

The world's most elusive criminal, Ilich Ramirez Sanchez, who avoided capture for 30 years, was sentenced to life imprisonment by a French court. The 48-year-old revolutionary assassin was unapologetic and declared himself a political prisoner. He believed that the deaths of the 80 people he murdered were necessary for 'the cause'. Interestingly the Palestine Liberation Army had severed contact with Carlos, 'because they actually believed in something' while the Jackal increasingly appeared to be simply enjoying his work. The Jackal's real name was Ilich Ramirez Sanchez and he was wanted for terrorist crimes in five European countries. He was born in Venezuela to a millionaire Marxist lawyer, who named his three sons Vladimir, Ilich and Lenin, after his Russian hero. The Jackal, so-named because of his ability to melt into shadows, was educated in Cuba, Moscow and London and was a linguist.

1818 James Joule, the English physicist, was born in Lancashire. The mechanical equivalent of a unit of heat, a joule, is named after him. He died in 1951.

1864 Australia's first major art gallery opened in Melbourne, Victoria.

1871 Giuseppe Verdi's opera *Aida* complete with extravagant props, such as live elephants and camels, premiered in Cairo, Egypt, to celebrate the opening of the Suez Canal.

1951 Libya gained its independence from France.

1995 Thousands of Palestinians gathered for the first time in 28-years to celebrate Christmas at Bethlehem's Manger Square, free from Israeli occupation. Palestine's president, Yasser Arafat, told the crowd and the world that 'Bethlehem, which is liberated, is the city of peace.'

Puerto Rican singer Ricky Martin performs at the Carousel of Hope, a star-studded charity gala benefitting childhood diabetes, in Beverly Hills, in October 2000.

25 DECEMBER

1946: Jimmy Buffett

The American country singer was born in Pascagoula, Mississippi. Raised in Mobile, Alabama he returned to Mississippi to go to college, where he took up the guitar 'to meet women.' He moved to Nashville to become a country star, but was only successful after he adopted a beach bum persona. His fans call themselves 'Parrotheads'. They wear beachcomber outfits with Hawaiian shirts and lei and follow Buffett around the country. Buffett's trademark song is 'Margaritaville'. He is a savvy businessman with a chain of clubs, a clothing line and a Margaritaville custom record label.

1977: Charlie Chaplin

The legendary comedian and movie director died aged 88. In 1960 he said, 'I remain just one thing and one thing only—and that is a clown.' Born into a very poor family in London, Chaplin was a vaudevillian who learned mime. With his brother Sidney he immigrated to America when Hollywood was just taking off. Chaplin first appeared in silent movies, becoming the iconic Tramp with his baggy pants, bowler hat, walking stick, little moustache and shuffling gait. He was an overnight success. At 29, he set up his own studio and was one of a trio who founded United Artists. In his autobiography he wrote, 'All I need to make a comedy is a park, a policeman and a pretty girl.' History has been kind to Sir Charles Spencer Chaplin, far kinder than the public and the media were in his lifetime. Among his greatest films were *The Gold Rush, Modern Times* and the *Great Dictator* in which he mocked Adolph Hitler. GB Shaw called him 'the one genius' of the movie industry. Winston Churchill praised him and Albert Einstein sought him out. His fourth and last marriage was happy although they lived in self-imposed exile in Switzerland. He and his wife Oona had eight children, including actress Geraldine Chaplin. In 1972, Hollywood finally acknowledged he had laid an incomparable comedy foundation since 1920 and he was honoured with an Oscar.

1859 Thomas Austin of Geelong, Victoria, released 72 partridges, 5 hares and 24 rabbits to aid food supply. Within years, rabbit-proof fences had to be built separating the states infested with them.

1917 To celebrate Christmas Day during World War I, a soccer game took place in France's Argonne Forest between the Allies and the Germans.

1957 Queen Elizabeth II delivered her first televised Christmas message to Commonwealth countries.

1983 Cabbage Patch Kids were the must-have Christmas present in America. The unique dolls came complete with adoption papers and no two were alike.

2001 More than 500 refugees stormed the French entrance to the English Chunnel in a desperate and unsuccessful attempt to reach England.

English actor and director Sir Charles Spencer Chaplin (1889–1977) in his classic dress, with Hollywood photographer Margaret Chute in 1935.

26 DECEMBER

2004: Boxing Day Tsunami

A devastating series of giant tidal waves hit eleven countries bordering the Indian Ocean without warning. A massive 9.0 magnitude earthquake off Aceh, Indonesia. triggered the deadly tsunami when continental plates shifted. More than 300 000 people died, largely in Southeast Asia, primarily in Indonesia, Sri Lanka, India and Thailand. The waves reached as far as Africa and claimed the lives of many European tourists. Entire villages were submerged and victims washed out to sea. Thousands were left destitute and the world responded with a widespread humanitarian effort. Over 100 aid agencies provided food, clean water, shelter, treated the injured, counselled the grief stricken and worked to prevent the outbreak of disease. Billions of dollars were donated by governments and individuals. The United Nations is working towards establishing an Indian Ocean tsunami warning system and there are proposals for a global warning system.

2004: Viktor Yushchenko

The Ukrainian Opposition candidate was elected Prime Minister, although the hotly contested ballot was not confirmed until early 2005. An election in November had declared current office holder, Viktor Yanukovich, the winner. Voters cried foul and demonstrated in crowds of hundreds of thousands for six weeks until the re-election was called. Vladimir Putin of Russia, who wanted to keep the former Soviet state less democratically governed, favoured Yanukovich. Doctors in Vienna confirmed that Viktor Yushchenko was poisoned by dioxin, in an attempt on his life, during the election campaign. He was seriously disfigured but survived. The plot was to kill him was attributed to the Yanukovich government and its Russian supporters, which incensed Ukrainians even more and made them determined to throw out the pro-Moscow government.

2004: The Trocks

Les Ballets Trockadero de Monte Carlo, the classical drag queen ballet dancers, celebrated their 30th anniversary in New York City. They combine ballet, cross-dressing and comedy. Wearing tutus and leaving their armpits unshaven, the ballerinas have both a male and a female persona. They have amusing names, such as Ida Nevasayneva and Vladimir Legupski. They are all professionally trained, superb dancers. The Trocks are the only male comedy dance company to be financially successful and have attracted a cult following.

1906 The world's first feature film, Australia's *The Story of the Kelly Gang*, premiered in Melbourne.

1909 Frederic Remington, the American cowboy artist and sculptor, died at age 48 from appendicitis. Theodore Roosevelt said that, 'He has portrayed a most characteristic and yet vanishing type of American life.'

1909 Dry Guzzlers: It was announced that the so-called 'dry' southern counties of America consumed more alcohol after the passage of legislation to limit alcohol consumption than before.

1928 Johnny Weissmuller retired from swimming to pursue his Tarzan movie career. He had not lost a freestyle amateur race in eight years. At one time, he held every world freestyle record from 50-yards to 880-yards.

1998 The annual Sydney-Hobart Yacht Race was devastated by a storm and six people died.

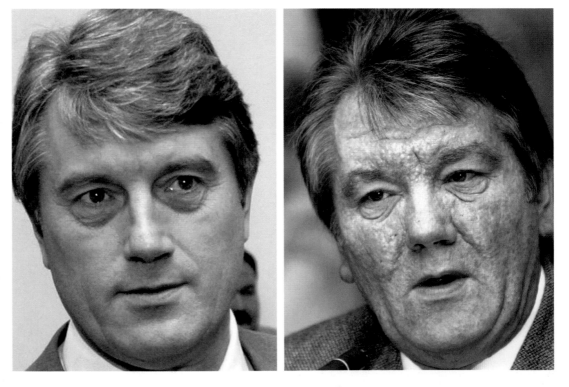

Two pictures of the Ukrainian opposition leader and then president Viktor Yushchenko .
Left: in Kiev 06 July 2004 and right: on 10 December 2004. Yushchenko was the victim of dioxin poisoning, his doctor in Vienna disclosed, adding that he suspected foul play. 'There is no doubt about the fact that the disease has been caused by a case of poisoning by dioxin,' said Dr Michael Zimpfer, the medical chief of Vienna's Rudolfinerhaus clinic.

27 DECEMBER

1803: Buckley's Mate

When Australians say, 'You've got Buckley's chance' they mean you've got no real chance. They're referring to the amazing adventures of the convict William Buckley, who escaped on this day from the Sydney penal settlement. Buckley was convicted of stealing cloth in England and sent to Australia as a convict. He escaped into the bush with five other convicts while the guards were sleeping. Hunger prompted the others to turn themselves in, but Buckley refused to give up. The Wathaurong Aborigines thought Buckley, with his white skin, was a reincarnated friend and took him in. They taught him to hunt, fish and thrive in the Australian bush. After 32 years of nomadic living Buckley rejoined the colony, became a guide and translator, helped establish Melbourne and was pardoned.

20044: Iran's Bam

The listing of Bam and its Cultural Landscape on UNESCO's World Heritage List and on the World Heritage List in Danger was celebrated on the first anniversary of the earthquake that destroyed much of the site and killed more than 26 000 people. Bam was a major crossroad on the ancient Silk Road, the important Asian trade route. Its fortified medieval city-fortress was the world's largest adobe building before the 2003 earthquake. Built sometime before 500 BC, it was abandoned in 1850 for unknown reasons. It is comprised of four sections and 36 watchtowers and is a phenomenal architectural feat. Rulers lived in areas separate from the middleclass and the poor. Wind towers provided ventilation by capturing wind and forcing it downward into the internal structures of the building. Underground irrigation canals are still used to provide water today. When the large gates to Bam were closed, the high walls and watchtowers provided protection. The entire city could be self-sustaining for long periods. Areas were devoted to cattle, gardens, gymnasiums, public baths, Mosques, stables, bakeries and bazaars.

1983: Pope John Paul II

The pontif met with the Turkish militant who shot him twice in the abdomen in May 1981. The man, Mehmet Ali Agca, who is serving a life sentence, fired on the Pope as he rode in his open car at St Peter's Square among a crowd of 10 000 worshippers. His assassin was an escaped prisoner. The Pope and his would-be-assassin spoke privately at the Italian prison where Agca was being held. The Pope said he regarded him, 'as a brother whom I have forgiven and who enjoys my confidence'.

1571 Johannes Kepler, one of the world's greatest astronomers, 'the father of modern astronomy' was born in Wurttemberg, Germany. He formulated the three laws of planetary motion. He died in 1630.

1822 Louis Pasteur, the chemist and bacteriologist, was born in the Jura, France. Food pasteurization techniques are named for him. He also successfully used the anti-rabies vaccine.

1836 England experienced its worst avalanche when eight people died in Lewes, Sussex.

1941 John Curtin, Australian Prime Minister, made his famous 'Australia looks to America' speech. Great Britain was too pre-occupied with the European and Southeast Asian theatres of War to help Australia, so Curtin appealed to the Americans for help against the Japanese.

1948 Gerard Depardieu, the French actor, was born in Chateauroux. He has appeared in many English speaking films, including *Green Card* and *Cyrano de Bergerac.*

French film stars Carole Bouquet and Gerard Depardieu pose at the World Economic Forum in Switzerland in 2005.

28 DECEMBER

1763: John Molson

The Canadian brewer was born. When he was orphaned in his late teens he emigrated from England to Montreal. In 1786, he founded Canada's most successful brewery, which still bears his name. He owned a fleet of 22 steamboats for the St Lawrence Waterway traffic. Molson became a very influential businessman, President of the Bank of Montreal, established the first iron foundry in Canada and built Montreal's first permanent theatre. With others, he founded Montreal General, the first public hospital. He was also one of the investors in the Champlain and St Lawrence Railroad.

1933: FDR

American President Franklin Delano Roosevelt (FDR) expanded on a prior speech by President Woodrow Wilson, proclaiming American neutrality in foreign incidents: 'The definite policy of the United States, from now on, is one opposed to armed intervention.' In 1941, he would, however, declare war on the Japanese after Pearl Harbour. Born in Hyde Park, New York on 30 January 1882, FDR was the American President from 1933-1945 and the only person to serve four terms. FDR contracted polio aged 39, but only used a wheelchair and braces in private, refusing to be photographed in his wheelchair. During the Depression, he said, 'The only thing we have to fear is fear itself,' and his economic and social programs, known as the New Deal, helped America regain stability. His presidency is filled with unparalleled milestones that helped establish the post-World War II world. Roosevelt died in 1945 at Warm Springs, Georgia, just weeks before the German surrender. His freethinking wife Eleanor, was known as 'First Lady of the World.'

1954: Denzel Washington

One of the major African-American actors of the 20th century was born in Mount Vernon, New York. Washington was banned from watching movies as a child. His first major role was in Wilma, during the filming of which he met his future wife, Pauletta Pearson. Washington won his first Oscar in 1989 for Best Supporting Actor in Glory. He studied boxing for over a year to play Rubin 'Hurricane' Carter in The Hurricane. In 1992 he starred in Malcolm X and was chosen by *People* magazine as one of the sexiest stars in movie history. Washington won his second Oscar for Best Actor in *Training Day*.

1869 William F Semple of Mount Vernon, Ohio, patented chewing gum.

1897 Edmond Rostand's classic play Cyrano de Bergerac premiered in Paris.

1934 English actress Dame Maggie Smith was born in Ilford, England. She is recognised as Britain's greatest living actress. She starred in *The Prime of Miss Jean Brodie, Lettuce and Lovage* and in the *Harry Potter* movies.

1957 The biggest abattoir in northern England shut down when foot-and-mouth disease was identified in cattle awaiting slaughter.

1984 Actor, writer and director Sam Peckinpah died aged 59. His movies include *Straw Dogs* and *The Wild Bunch*.

Denzel Washington and wife Pauletta at 'The 17th Annual American Cinematheque Award Honoring Denzel Washington' in Beverly Hills, California, in 2002.

29 DECEMBER

1809: William Gladstone

The four-times British Prime Minister was born in Liverpool, England. He alternated the post with his political rival Benjamin Disraeli. They had enormous dislike for each other. Disraeli once said, 'Gladstone, like (French Cardinal) Richelieu can't write. Nothing can be more unmusical, more involved or more uncouth than all his scribblement.' Gladstone was either intensely loved or hated by the public and wherever he went there were cheers, or jeers. He died in 1898 in Hawarden, Wales. His rival, the Italian-Jewish Conservative Disraeli, was Prime Minister in 1868 and from 1874-80. Disraeli was very close to Queen Victoria who tolerated his eccentricities and his frequent outlandish foppishness. The journalist and Labour politician Michael Foot wrote about Disraeli, 'He was without rival whatever, the first comic genius whoever installed himself in Downing Street.'

1967: Andy Wachowski

The film producer was born in Chicago. With his older brother Larry, the Wachowskis have revolutionised sci-fi movies, with their *Matrix* and *Animatrix* series. The brothers were always avid science fiction fans and dropped out of college to devote their time to screenwriting. Combining martial arts, action and cyber-noir visuals the brothers wrote and produced the *Matrix* series. It was an overnight sensation, winning four Oscars. *The Matrix Reloaded* and *The Matrix Revolutions* followed. Filmed in Australia, the *Matrix* series explore humankind's fight to reclaim control of its destiny. The Wachowski brothers live private lives, refusing to promote their movies, preferring that their movies speak for themselves.

1972: Jude Law

The British actor was born in London. Some people speculate that he was named after the Beatles' song 'Hey Jude,' but his birth name is David Jude Law. He started acting at 12 and at 17 dropped out of school just prior to graduation to star in the television soap opera *Families*. After successfully acting on stage, Law's first major film role was in the movie *Shopping*. He also appeared in *The Talented Mr. Ripley, Cold Mountain* and *Alfie*. Law is particular about accepting roles based on his desire not to be typecast in romantic roles by his good looks and English accent. He is a partner in the production company Natural Nylon and divides his time between producing and acting. In 2004, Jude Law was named *People* magazine's 'Sexiest Man Alive.'

1900 Ice Hockey great Nels Stewart was born in Montreal. He was the first hockey pro to score 300 goals. He holds the record for the fastest hockey goals—two in four seconds.

1916 Grigori Rasputin was poisoned, shot and drowned, aged 45. He was accused of having too much power over the Russian Tsar and his family.

1946 Marianne Faithfull, the singer and actress, was born in London and was one of the first English female rock stars of the 1960s. Her signature song is 'As Tears Go By.'

1986 Harold Macmillan, the former British Prime Minister, died aged 92.

1989 Vaclav Havel, the playwright and former political prisoner, became Czechoslavakian president in the 'Velvet Revolution.' He left office after thirteen years.

2000 Cricket history was made when Australia won thirteen consecutive Test matches.

Jude Law (left), Sienna Miller and Michael Caine at a screening of *Casablanca* in London in 2005.

30 DECEMBER

1865: Rudyard Kipling

The British author was born in Bombay, India. He became England's first Nobel Laureate for Literature in 1907 and is best known for writing *The Man Who Would Be King*, *Kim*, *Just So Stories* and *The Jungle Book*. He coined many phrases, such as 'the white man's burden' and 'East is East and West is West and never the twain shall meet.' He gave his babysitter a manuscript and said it, 'might be worth holding onto and selling one day.' She sold *The Jungle Book* and was able to live comfortably for the rest of her life. Kipling died in 1936 in London and is buried in Poet's Corner in Westminster Abbey.

1869: Steven Leacock

The author was born in Swanmore, Hampshire England, the third in a family of 11 children. They immigrated to South Africa, then to America before settling in rural Canada. Leacock's primary interest was in political science and economics, but his humourous writing and biographies of Mark Twain and Charles Dickens brought him widespread acclaim, as did his radio shows and speaking tours. His *Literary Lapses*, a compilation of his humourous writings, established him as a major and prolific author. In 1944, he died of throat cancer in Toronto. His unfinished autobiography, *The Boy I Left Behind*, was published posthumously. Today, his home is a historic site, museum and memorial. The Stephen Leacock Medal for Humour is awarded yearly for the best humourous book by a Canadian author. In 1998, the University of Toronto published Leacock's doctoral dissertation *The Doctrine of Laissez-faire*. Leacock had submitted it 94 years earlier. He would have found that humourous.

1997: Sir Elton John

Buckingham Palace announced that Elton John, one of the most successful pop singers, would be knighted. Born in 1947 in Pinner, England with the birth name Reginald Dwight, he combined the names of two of his favourite artists, Elton Dean and John Baldry to become Elton John. He began playing piano aged four years old. The pop megastar is known for his glamrock flamboyant costumes and matching glasses. For 30 years his hits topped the charts with songs like 'Rocket Man', 'Bennie and the Jets' and 'I Guess That's Why They Call It the Blues'. He was inducted into the Rock and Roll Hall of Fame in 1994. In 1995 he won a Grammy for 'Can You Feel the Love Tonight' and he rewrote 'Candle in the Wind' for Princess Diana's funeral in 1997.

1928 Singer, songwriter, guitarist Bo 'The Originator' Diddley was born in McCombs, Mississippi. His signature song is 'I'm A Man.' He continues to produce explosive music, such as 'A Man Amongst Men'.

1959 Comedian and stage and screen actress Tracey Ullman was born in Slough, England. She has won six Emmys. Her zany television show, which ran for four years, was based on the scores of characters she created.

1982 Actress, model Kristen Kreuk was born in Vancouver, Canada. The half-Dutch, half-Chinese actress starred in *Edgemont* and TV's *Smallville*.

2002 American psychologist Eleanor Gibson died aged 92. She pioneered work in babies' perception and was one of the few psychologists to receive the National Medal of Science.

Sir Elton John performs at Shoreline Amphitheatre in 1995 in Mountain View California.

31 DECEMBER

New Year's Eve: a traditional night for celebrating the arrival of a new year.

1700: Auld Lang Syne

Should auld acquaintance be forgot and never brought to mind? Should auld acquaintance be forgot and days of auld lang syne!
For auld lang syne, my dear, for auld lang syne, we'll take a cup 'o kindness yet, for auld lang syne.

The song Auld Lang Syne (Old Times Gone By) is sung at midnight on New Year's Eve all around the western world. It is a traditional Scottish song dating back to the 1700s, translated and brought to life by Scottish poet Robert Burns. In Scotland, New Year is called Hogmanay and in some villages barrels of tar are set alight and rolled through the streets. Thus, the old year is burned up and the new one allowed to enter. Scottish people believe that the first person to enter your house in the New Year will bring good or bad luck and it is especially lucky if the visitor is a dark-haired man bringing a gift. This custom is called first-footing.

1994: Biggest Party

Rod Stewart, the rock 'n roller with a gravelly voice, performed at the biggest outdoor concert in world history. The English star entertained a crowd estimated at 4.2 million on Copacabana Beach in Rio de Janiero, Brazil. 'Rod the Mod' started his career singing flops like 'Good Morning Little Schoolgirl' with Long John Baldry's Hoochie Coochie Men in 1964. He first tasted real success with the Jeff Beck Group when their album *Truth* hit the charts on both sides of the Atlantic. In the 1970s he joined Ron Wood and Ronnie Lane's The Faces before embarking on a solo career with his *Every Picture Tells a Story* album and its huge hit 'Maggie May.' He went through a disco phase and in the 1990s won new fans with his album *Unplugged … and seated*. By the millennium he was singing songs ol' Blue Eyes Frank Sinatra had popularised, with a series of albums called *The Great American Songbook*. Some of the songs are over eighty years old, but Stewart's fans have stuck with him. He has released more than twenty albums and sold in excess of 130 million records. He is still considered sexy at 60-years-old, enjoys life and still plays soccer. Stewart was inducted into the Rock and Roll Hall of Fame in 2004 .

1788 The Aboriginal Arabanoo was captured by Captain Arthur Phillip of the New South Wales convict colony to train him as an interpreter soon after the arrival of the First Fleet. He nursed two sick children back to good health after smallpox, before he fell victim himself and died in May 1789. Arabanoo was buried in the Governor's garden (now the Museum of Sydney).

1869 Artist Henri Matisse was born at Le Cateau, France. In 1961, his *Le Bateau* was hung upside down at a New York City exhibit and only after 47 days and 120 000 admirers did someone say, 'Oops. It's upside down!'

1943 Sir Ben Kingsley, the actor, was born Krishna Bhanji in Yorkshire, England of Indian (Gujarati) and Russian-Jewish descent. He won an Oscar for *Gandhi*. He also starred in *Schindler's List*, *Turtle Diary* and *House of Sand and Fog* and was knighted in 2001.

1980 Canada's Marshall McLuhan died on a cold winter day in Toronto. He once said, 'most people are alive in an earlier time, but you must be alive in our own time.'

2004 The 100th anniversary of New York City's Times Square Ball, that gives the countdown to midnight.

Actor Sir Ben Kingsley attends the premiere of the film *Triumph Of Love* in 2002 in Hollywood.

INDEX